A Herstory of Transmasculine Identities

An Annotated Anthology

Contributors

Bobbi Aubin ✦ Caden Rocker ✦ Maxwell Alderdice ✦
Day Walker ✦ Tygh Lawrence-Clark ✦ Shawn L. ✦
Tristan Rounkles ✦ Stephen Ostrow ✦ Lucas Aiden Wehle ✦
L.W. Lucas Hasten ✦ Hunter T. ✦ Lee Harrington ✦
Avi Ben-Zeev ✦ Max Meyer ✦ Jackson Jantzen ✦ Evan R. ✦
Cooper Lee Bombardier

Michael Eric Brown

Foreword by Joe Ippolito, PsyD., LICSW

. Published by
Boundless Endeavors, Inc.

Printed in the United States of America

Published by Boundless Endeavors, Inc.
2250 NW 114th Place Unit 1P, PTY 21068
Miami, FL 33179
www.boundlessendeavors.com

First Printing, 2016

Library of Congress Control Number: 2016904273
ISBN-13: 978-0-9968309-2-8 (print)
ISBN-10: 0-9968309-2-8 (print)
ISBN-13: 978-0-9968309-3-5 (e-book)
ISBN-10: 0-9968309-3-6 (e-book)

Includes bibliographical references.

Reviews

A Herstory of Transmasculine Identities is a provocative and important exploration of trans men's experiences and identities. It's an important addition to the discussion of transfeminist experiences and politics, and it's an important addition to a growing canon of works exploring transfeminist experiences and politics.
– **Masen Davis, co-director of *Global Action for Trans Equality***

⬥⬥⬥

Michael Eric Brown calls *A Herstory of Transmasculine Identities: An Annotated Anthology,* reflecting the fact that the book is an anthology but also so much more. It's fitting that a book about the non-binary diversity of trans-masculine identities itself refuses to conform to traditional boundaries and definitions. That is to say, *A Herstory of Transmasculine Identities* is part anthology, part memoir, part Trans 101, part academic exploration of masculine identities attached to bodies assigned female at birth. This book is particularly important because it gives voice to those whose masculine identities aren't reflected in traditional forms. Those who identify as butch, bois, genderqueer, gender variant, gender-fluid—sometimes even as they also identify as women or lesbians—rarely find their lives reflected in print. Brown brings a trans masculine feminist perspective to reflective questions about gender and sexuality and accepts what others might find incongruent, including that trans men have herstories to embrace.
– **Jacob Anderson-Minshall, co-author *Queerly Beloved: A Love Story Across Genders.***

⬥⬥⬥

Michael Eric Brown and several other authors have added a valuable work to the literature of genderqueer and transgender theory. *A Herstory of Transmasculine Identities: An Annotated Anthology* argues that there is an unexamined need for many female-to-male trans individuals to continue to honor a past connection to the lesbian community, and for the lesbian community to cease to excommunicate those whose path takes them beyond butch and across the line into the world of embodied trans identity. It includes several moving memoirs from differently-gendered people who cannot be shoehorned into traditional male or female categories. Brown's arguments are controversial and complex, stretching the relatively new field of trans-scholarship in important ways. These are issues that need to be discussed with less rancor and more open-minded curiosity.
– Patrick Califia, author of *Sex Changes: The Politics of Transgenderism*

※※※

We all have stories to tell. These stories form the fabric of our identity. Each person who embarks on a journey to explore their felt gender identity has made a commitment to authenticity. Authenticity is not always highly valued in society; which makes the decision to embark on this journey all the more important. This book offers an important glimpse into the lives of trans masculine people as they explore their identity in a manner that brings to the fore the stark reality of what is means to live in one's truth.
–*lore m. dickey, PhD.* Assistant Professor and Training Director, *Northern Arizona University*

※※※

Table of Contents

Foreword

"The personal is political" – This rallying slogan has resonated strongly in my psyche for over 30 years. It started when I was about 9 years old, after I accompanied my mother to work at the "clinic." This was no ordinary "clinic". It was actually a place where women – who were pregnant, but opted not to keep their child – could safely terminate the pregnancy. Mother told me "not all women" want to and/or can give birth to and keep their babies and this was okay. Even at this young age, I understood and digested what she was saying, and over time, grew into the feminist ally I consider myself to be today.

For over a decade, I have been waiting to read a book like *A Herstory of Transmasculine Identities*. As a 46-year-old trans man, who was actively part of lesbian and feminist communities for 15 years prior to transition, many of the theories and phenomenological experiences presented in this book hit home.

From the moment I started reading Chapter 1, *What's Up With Herstory When We Are Men?* through to the end, these words echoed some of my own experiences. Unlike other books written about the trans masculine experience, I could truly relate to what the author, Michael Eric Brown, and some of the contributors had to say about the intersection of trans masculine identity, feminist community and lesbian culture. While this book may only address the experiences of a certain segment of trans men, these candid voices need to be heard, as opposed to pushed into the corner like they have been for far too long.

For so many of the contributors, their identities as trans men, connection to women communities and dedication to the feminist movement have been questioned and ridiculed. .

One particular chapter, *The Love That Remains,* by Cooper Lee Bombardier spoke to me. Not only am I currently the same age as Cooper, but I, too, was part of 1990s dyke culture. While Cooper experienced this in San Francisco, I had a comparable one in New York City. Cooper hung out at "Muff Dive," a well-known San Francisco dyke bar and I spent my "dyke nights out" dancing at "Meow Mix" on the Lower East Side of Manhattan.

Another chapter that caught my eye was, *Being Myself,* by Caden

Rocker. While Caden is 14 years younger than me, we both lived as lesbians for a significant period of our lives. Upon transitioning into men, we were accused by lesbian friends of being "sell outs" or giving into the patriarchy. On the flip side, entrance into the "trans" world came with its own set of costs, and like Caden, I continue to see the process of transition as a journey that never really stops.

Anyone interested in learning more about the diverse evolution of the trans masculine experience, as well as opening their minds to another way of seeing things need to read this book. Like Brown states at the end of Part 1, it's time to open up our minds and hearts to the finding our true voices and truths, even if that voice comes from a trans masculine person who identifies as a trans man, relates to feminist ideologies, and continues to connect to lesbian community.

Joe Ippolito, PsyD., LICSW
Trans Man & Feminist Ally

Preface

I am a trans man. Notice the modifier—*trans*. I was assigned female at birth because of my genitalia, but, living as a girl and then as a woman for nearly forty years of my life did not convince me that I "fit" into the mold of *woman*. After sixteen years of living on the 'other' side, in a socially-constructed role of a *man*, I can say without hesitation that my experiences of being socialized as a woman created every facet of the person I am today. I will never be a biological 'male,' whether I wish for it or not—and I do not wish for it. If I had been born assigned male at birth, I would not have the experiences of what it is like to be the 'oppressed,' and without these experiences, I would have no second thoughts about being a member of this patriarchal society. I cannot, and will not, ever renounce my female past; for it is because of it that I am a caring, considerate, strong and compassionate feminist man who does everything within his power to make life just a little less scary, a little less complicated, and a little less oppressed for women and gender non-conforming individuals.

I founded TransMentors International, Inc. several years ago in order to provide support to trans-identified individuals. I had been mentoring young FTMs prior to forming the non-profit organization, and realized how desperately we all need support during what can be considered the most difficult time in our lives—coming out as a trans person. I have seen the fears, the losses and the depression—and I have seen the growth into authentic selves and the excitement that comes with it. I have also seen the sadness and grief when some realize they have left the only community they knew, and they are subsequently rejected by other trans individuals because they present or perform their gender differently than others.

I have seen my share of the stories of murders and suicides of trans individuals, people who were simply trying to live their lives authentically and were cut short because of discrimination—harassment, bullying, abuse, and violence—and I've seen the grief and the anger of those left behind. I wrote a short play called *On Passing* in 2013 (published in 2015), about a young college-age man who lived stealth, had a girlfriend, and was pursuing a degree in psychology—only to have his life brutally ended because of hate and bigotry. The reactions I received from those who read the script convinced me that I could do more; I could continue to share the truth and shed light on the realities of being a trans individual through writing.

I continued to write my truth, and published my book, *Pencil Me In: A Trans Perspective in a Gendered World* in 2015. In it, I gave a first-hand account of my life as a trans individual, growing up in a home that was loaded with abuse, and the ensuing anger and depression that followed for many years, well into my many years in the LGBT community. It came to a point in my life where I was either going to end my life and be one of the statistics, or I was going to take the leap and start living my life authentically. I chose the latter, but have never forgotten what that depression feels like or what the discrimination and abuse felt like—because in choosing to remember, I am charged with passion and energy to continue doing my part in helping other trans-identified individuals through their own emotional and physical rollercoasters of gender and sexual identities.

This book was borne of hundreds of conversations and observations through the years with other transmasculine individuals—some identify as FTM (female-to-male), while others think of themselves as transsexual, or transgender, genderqueer, gender non-conforming, two-spirit, bigender, omnigender, gender-fluid, and a number of other self-identifying terminologies. It is intended to put a spotlight on a certain group of these individuals who came from lesbian and/or feminist backgrounds because, in my observations, conversations, and subsequent research I have found that these are people who have come from a place which consisted of a strong female community or they have embraced their female pasts as an integral part of who they are today. Not all were as committed to the lesbian or feminist communities as others, but none are not ashamed of having *herstory* (which is a word that will be defined and explained in detail within Part I). Many of these, too, are the individuals who experience a 'disconnect' in the greater transmasculine community, because of the rigid gender 'rules' perceived and imposed by those who have rejected their female past, sometimes to the extreme point of rejecting all things feminine.

The individuals who have contributed to this anthology are tired of staying silent and dissatisfied with not being able to share their backgrounds for fear of discrimination, or being made fun of, or being rejected in social media groups due to their beliefs, their values, and their acceptance of from where they came. Some just needed a chance to share their stories. Not all came from a lesbian or feminist background and not all are heterosexual; but each acknowledges their past—the good and the bad. Each of these individuals are doing their part in trying to educate the community and society at large on the fact that the trans community is incredibly diverse within itself and that we are all valid and valuable human beings that deserve honor, dignity and respect from all other human beings.

I invite you to read this book in its entirety, Part I and Part II, with an open and discerning mind. If you choose to skip reading Part I because you are only interested in the personal stories in Part II, you will have missed the opportunity to understand how each of the stories reflect on vital components of the terminologies, issues and concerns found in Part I. In reading the stories alone, you will have disadvantaged and deprived yourself of the deeper meanings and significance behind their words.

I am a trans man. And, I am a part of this wonderful world of gender and sexual diversity.

Michael Eric Brown
2016

Acknowledgements

Without the support of a few significant people in my life, this book would not have come to fruition, and I would be remiss if I did not give credit where it belongs.

Always first and foremost is my wife, Lillian, who has from the beginning of our life together, stood beside me and been supportive and encouraging of me. I am so incredibly fortunate, and am humbled by her unconditional love for me—for loving the person I am, exactly the way I am. Not a day goes by without me stopping for a moment to reflect on the joy she gives me just by being herself.

Although the intention in the beginning was to co-author this book with Jackson Jantzen, things don't always work out as planned because, well, sometimes life just gets in the way. Jackson's constructive comments throughout the writing process, however, have been invaluable in the preparation of this book, and it would not be the same without his indispensable contributions. He was adept at analyzing each chapter paragraph by paragraph to make sure they flowed smoothly and clearly, pointing out where improvements could be made. Jackson also contributed a chapter, sharing his story which is one that is similarly shared by so many in the transmasculine community, those who began their journey to authenticity in the lesbian community.

Without Sam Waters, I am afraid you would be putting up with various punctuation issues. Although I am fairly good at proofreading, I falter when it comes to correct placement of periods and commas when anywhere near a quotation mark (other than for an APA citation). Sam has spent a good number of hours proofreading this book to make certain it will be accepted by even the most scrutinizing readers.

I want to also acknowledge the Artist who created the main cover graphic, Marval Rechsteiner, a.k.a. Marval A. Rex. I came across Marval during my research, and upon reading the story of his top surgery, I asked him for permission to quote him in the book, and you'll it in find in Chapter 6. His eagerness to help further, and his artistic skill, led to an abundance of emails to conceive of and create an image that best fit what I had envisioned. The "kaleidoscope" appearance emanating outwards from the center is meant to show the intersections and connections in a person's life, and with the chaos all around, there is completeness; a valid, whole human being in the middle of it all. You'll find, too, in Chapter 1 the mention of a "kaleidoscope" of terminologies and identities.

To the trans men and feminist pioneers who came before me, especially those who recorded your experiences and your research to share with the world, I thank you. It is because of your courage and your many academic, professional and personal writings that I draw upon for personal learning experience. Some of you will find yourselves quoted in Part I, because your words and ideas are important and necessary for the continued education of those willing to learn.

Most importantly, I acknowledge my community of trans brothers and sisters. My life is dedicated to all of you, and I hope in some way through this book, my other writings and through my organization, TransMentors International, that I can help make a difference in your lives, or provide inspiration to those who are out there advocating on our behalf to make our world a better place.

Brief Introduction

I am fully aware that not all who read books choose to read the Introduction, preferring rather to skip right to the first chapter and the heart of the matter. Because of this reality, I have chosen to keep this Introduction concise by sharing the three most important points I wish to convey to you; I will provide further, in-depth detail in Chapter 1 and beyond.

1.   This book has been written for one purpose: To educate and inform those who want to learn about the diversity within the trans male community, using empirical, academic and phenomenological research, as well as through original essay contributions from men who want their stories to be heard.

2.   This book *does not in any way* represent the lives of all transmasculine individuals. It is intended to portray a segment of the trans male community whose voices have not yet been heard, and are many times misunderstood. This book has provided an opportunity for some these individuals to speak out about their lives and experiences and is intended to foster education for those who want to learn more about this facet of the community.

3.   The word 'herstory' is not reflecting or implying that trans men are female or identify as such. It is a word that certain transmasculine individuals embrace because they have come from being assigned a female at birth; some followed the path of lesbianism and gained strong feminist backgrounds prior to proclaiming their identity as male, while others did not do either; but these individuals do agree that their time in the socially constructed role of "woman" gave them herstory. This latter category of individuals includes those who may have lived as straight, cisgender (non-trans) women and once transitioned to male continued with the same sexual orientation of preferring male sexual partners, so are now considered gay. They all have herstory to share.

There is more depth to these statements and definitions which will be uncovered and explained further while you are reading through this book. I hope you find this annotated anthology both educational and enlightening in your path to discovering the lives of these men and this facet of our community. My wish is that when you finish reading, you will have gained an appreciation and validation for those whose stories might be considered controversial by some.

The book is divided into two parts. Part I has been provided as an educational resource, while Part II contains the stories from transmasculine individuals who wish to share their experiences with you. Some will share their names, while others prefer to use a pseudonym. Additionally, scattered throughout the various chapters and within the annotations, you will find quotations from individuals who either wish to remain anonymous, or their experiences were shared during my research where anonymity was an expectation and guaranteed. In the latter, there is no information shared which infringes upon the personal privacy of these individuals.

Part I

Reflecting on Diversity

We must learn from the past if we are to be able to engage creatively with the present ~ V.J. Siedler, 2006, p. xix

What's Up With Herstory
When We Are Men?

Every man is more than just himself; he also represents the unique, the very special and always significant and remarkable point at which the world's phenomena intersect, only once in this way, and never again. That is why every man's story is important, eternal, sacred; that is why every man, as long as he lives and fulfills the will of nature, is wondrous, and worthy of consideration ~ Hermann Hesse (1877-1962)

To reiterate the words in the Brief Introduction (you did read it, right?): *This book is not intended in any way to be a representation of all transgender men or transmasculine individuals.* None of these stories characterize or describe the entire Transmasculine community, nor does any one story or all of them collectively represent a full history for the greater majority of transmen.

I feel it is important to address the intended reasoning for publishing this book and to provide a clear definition of those to whom I am giving a voice. It is also important to understand definitions as well as to recognize the importance and significance of personal self-identification in the trans community. I have chosen to use this first chapter due to the propensity of some to avoid reading book Introductions. Consider this chapter the full Introduction.

The text and stories communicated here are about a specific segment of transmen in the community whose stories and lives reflect certain experiences that *not all trans men encounter or undergo.* This book is for them and about them. It is designed to give a voice and a platform for them to share their lives with you, the Reader, and to broaden our collective understanding of all the wondrous diverse identities that make up our community.

※※※※

My first serious long-term partner, Lee, was a very assertive and masculine female-bodied person. I was twenty-five years younger than her forty-eight years, just barely out in the world on my own in my early twenties when we met. It was the beginning of the 1980s, and I was living among the gay and lesbian community in a progressive Pacific Northwest college town. The other letters in the rainbow acronym hadn't quite come to be used popularly, so we were not yet using GLBT or LGBT as a standard.

Lee self-identified as a male as well as a transgender man, and had lived and worked as one for most of her (yes, I said 'her'—don't panic!) adult life, nearly twenty-five years of it; however, she preferred people in her social life to refer to her with female pronouns. She lived socially as a lesbian, having come from a seventeen-year long relationship with another lesbian at the time we met; prior to that she had her time of living wild and free in the late Fifties and early Sixties with countless women she had bedded through the years. She had also married out of high school, and had borne two children.

Lee spoke of her history, which she called *herstory*, a term created by Robin Morgan and later used in her book "*Sisterhood is Powerful*" (1970, p. 551), and then later by other feminists. I had the privilege of hearing and learning first-hand from someone who had lived and was actively demonstrating during the Civil Rights Movement as well as through the emergence of the Second Wave of Feminism. The year we began our relationship, Coretta Scott King announced her support of the Gay Civil Rights Movement, and the previous decade or two had celebrated enormous victories for women on several crucial platforms.

I had been involved in a local *Take Back the Night* march a few years prior to meeting her and many of my friends, both lesbian and non-lesbians, were formidable feminists, so the term *herstory* was not new to me. Nor did I ever question its authenticity or importance since it was used by those who defined themselves and their past with this term.

Lee chose to speak of her own herstory as a transmasculine individual because of her self-identification as lesbian and as a feminist. This did not make her any less of a man, nor any greater of a woman. We were not advantaged in those days of having the means of instant communication and education via the internet, so we had not yet recognized fully the fluidity or immenseness of gender and sexuality. We simply accepted that all human beings have a right to identify in any way they feel comfortable, and it was not up to anyone else to dispute this fact.

Through the following decades, our language of sex and gender has evolved into a kaleidoscope of terminologies and identities. If Lee were around today, she would feel blessed to know that she was not the only one who followed a path similar to her own. It is the purpose of this chapter to try to convey the simplicities and complexities of a more often than not hidden and silent group of individuals with a *transmasculine identity* and *herstory*.

✖✖✖

What Is "Herstory"?

The word *herstory* arrived into contemporary English language with a slight change of the beginning letters of the word 'history' to *her*, creating a word that has nothing to do with perceived male pronouns. Some individuals have embraced this word over the years using it to describe their backgrounds and signifying their autonomy and resilience in our male-dominated society.

One dictionary defines *herstory* as "history considered or presented from a feminist viewpoint or with special attention to the experience of women" (Herstory, n.d.). According to Currie and Rothenberg, "The focus is on the self-definition of the individual woman, not of the group, and yet the union with other women is the foundation of that ability to self-define....Herstory accomplishes interdependent self-actualization" (2002). Lastly, Jane Mills stated about substituting the word history with *herstory* that it was "guaranteed to annoy most men, many women and almost all linguists" (1989, p. 118). It continues to be used in contemporary times; including in blogs, books and academic journals. I must note, however, that there is no mention that the term *herstory* can only be claimed by women; it simply means *history from a feminist viewpoint*.

Before I can explain how the term *herstory* applies to transmasculine identities, I believe it is first necessary to address the definitions and broader intersections of *gender, sexuality,* and *masculinity,* and how *feminism* relates to each. This chapter will give a brief synopsis of each, while later chapters here in Part I will examine each in greater depth.

Breaking Down Gender

The ideas and concepts of gender have caused confusion for many, yet we all have one whether or not we think about it, vocalize it or portray it in some way or other. Different cultures define gender in various ways, and not all of them subscribe to the popular notion of "pink is for girls" and "blue is for boys." It is not uncommon to see men wearing pink or carrying pastel-colored accessories in Latin American countries, for instance. Prior to the 1950s in the United States, pink and blue, were not yet widely used as defining colors for boys and girls. "There was no gender-color symbolism that held true everywhere" (Wolchover, 2012, para. 2).

John Money (1955) defined gender and sex as being separate, and broadened the definition of gender into more than just masculine and feminine. Nicolson (1994, p. 80) suggested that gender was *causally constructed*, meaning that social forces have a role in our existence—they shape the way we become men and women. By the late 1960s, in order to explain why some people felt that they were 'trapped in the wrong bodies' Stoller (1968), like Money before him, differentiated the two words by referring to 'sex' for the biological traits and 'gender' to point out, in his assessment, the amount of femininity and masculinity a person exhibits.

✖✖✖

> *Editor Note: There is a plethora of studies that indicate children are aware of gender, gender roles, and stereotypes well before they reach the age of five, including having the ability to define their own gender identity. This subject of youth, is left to the many other publications available, however, as it is far too encompassing to write more about this here and does not coincide with the purpose of this book.*

Around the same time Stoller was announcing his theory, feminists, too, began distinguishing between sex and gender, which supported their argument that many of the differences between men and women were "socially produced, and, therefore, changeable" (Mikkola, 2016, Sec. 1.2, para. 2). Judith Butler said genders are "true and real only to the extent that they are performed" (1980, p. 527). Mikkola follows this line of reasoning with the statement "Without heterosexism that compels people to engage in certain gendering acts, there would not be any genders at all" (2012, sec. 3.12, para. 5). This *performance* of gender is what some people refer to as "Doing gender", a term first coined by Candace West and Don H. Zimmerman in 2009.

There is a well-known and often-used saying that has become widely used in gender rhetoric first stated by Virginia Prince in 1971, "Any kind of carving that you might do on me might change my sex, but it would not change my gender, because *my gender, my self-identity, is between my ears, not between my legs*" (emphasis added). Although somewhat simplistic in nature, its effect is profound in promoting understanding for those who continuously conflate the two. "The implication is that, while sex is immutable, gender is something individuals have control over – it is something we can alter and change through individual choices" (Mikkola, 2012, sec. 3.4, para. 2).

With the awareness of the above definitions, and by thinking of gender as a *performance*, we can then formulate an educated assertion: Gender, being a social construct, is simply not binary—there are no longer just two genders, male and female—but rather a continuum of gender identities. If one were a mathematician, one would say there are an infinite number of identities between the endpoints of male and female since all individuals have self-identified to some degree in one direction or another. Or sometimes both, or even none.

Those who have "crossed" genders are generally considered *transgender* individuals (*trans* meaning "cross", "across", "beyond" or "through", depending upon the dictionary one chooses to consult or the individual defining it). Many individuals consider themselves to be under the *transgender umbrella*. This term was created to encompass all traditional gender non-conforming individuals; including *transsexual, transgender, genderqueer, gender fluid, bi-gender, multi-gender, two-spirit, intersex, non-binary, androgynous* and several more identity terms. Some people embrace and regularly use the term *transgender umbrella*, while others do not perceive themselves as being "under the umbrella."

Susan Stryker's definition of transgender in her book *Transgender History* (2008, p. 1) sums it up efficiently when she writes, "It is the movement across a socially imposed boundary away from an unchosen starting place— rather than any particular destination or mode of transition— that best characterizes the concept of 'transgender' ". Some individuals prefer to use the abbreviated term *trans*, while others add an asterisk at the end *trans** in an attempt to widen the net for the embracement all gender identities.

There are those who embrace the word *transsexual*, or the phrase a person of *transsexual experience* to describe themselves, while others do not use any variation of the term *trans*. In Aaron (nee: Holly) Devor's study in 1997, it was found that after a gender transition there were FTMs who "lived their lives as unremarkable men whose transsexuality remained invisible except to specifically chosen other people. They treated the information that they once had been female and had lived as girls and as women as potentially discrediting information which needed to be managed with care" (p. 604). I mention this because it is important to note that for many years, transsexuals were expected to blend into society. There are some who did so many years ago, only to more recently begin living more openly, and many of those choose to continue to use the term *transsexual* or a person with *transsexual experience*.

Can Gender and Sexuality Be Combined Somehow?

Despite all I have said above, that gender and sex are two separate entities, in a simple answer I undeniably have to say *yes, sometimes*; there are those individuals who consider themselves transmen (the gender), and also choose to claim the sexual identity of lesbian (the sexuality). In my research, and throughout my adult life, I have found and known several who embrace both identities. One FTM states with confidence, "I identify as a lesbian and a dyke, so it doesn't seem that strange to me. We all get to choose labels that feel good to us." Another identifies as a *socially masculine-identified genderqueer* and says that he is okay with *butch* in the queer word, but in the straight world he is *male*. One says he does not identify as a lesbian but instead as queer, even though he prefers women as partners. He does not think of himself as straight, although he describes himself as a very binary masculine man.

The idea of transmen claiming the sexual identity of *lesbian* can be explained by thinking in terms of *lesbian* not being just a clinical (or dictionary) description. The term *lesbian* generally denotes a woman who prefers women as intimate sexual partners; but it is also a culture and collection of experiences.

Others, however, emphatically exclaim that men cannot claim the identity of lesbian, and state "Someone cannot just take a word and do whatever they want with it. Men cannot be lesbians, it's a farce and not credible." However, if one were to consider that there are *at least* two "categories" of FTMs (and we know there are more), with one being non-binary, one must also consider the possibility that a person could potentially identify as a trans man yet embrace his lesbian identity. *It does not need to fit neatly into a dictionary definition.*

Susan Stryker wrote "Gendering practices are inextricably enmeshed with sexuality. The identity of the desiring subject and that of the object of desire are characterized by gender" (2014, p. 39). Hansbury, in his attempt to describe how individuals identify, indicated how "Someone may identify as a Transsexual Man yet still maintain his breasts and forego testosterone. Another may choose to undergo a mastectomy, take low-dosage testosterone, and identify as a Passing Woman" (2004, p. 245)

There are those in the trans community who prefer not to use the typical pronouns of *he, his, she, and her*, etc. Some prefer only the pronouns of *they* and *them*. Author and activist Leslie Fienberg (1949–2014) identified as a butch lesbian and a transgender lesbian who liked the gender neutral pronouns of *ze* and *hir*, but would also accept the traditional pronouns depending on the context of the setting at the time (Feinberg, 2006). Nearly every trans individual accepts the variation of pronouns, and adopts those which are comfortable for themselves. *What, then, makes any identity that one might embrace seem a threat to others?*

I will be going more into depth on gender in Chapter 2, but I also wish invite you to research this topic further or contact us with your sincere questions.

❀❀❀

> *Every human being has the right to define himself, herself, or their self in any way they are comfortable and be free from recrimination and discrimination from not only society as a whole, but also within their own community of other trans individuals. This includes the identities of gender and sexuality as well as sexual orientation.* ~
> Michael Eric Brown

Transmasculine Identities

Transmasculine identities is the term I have chosen to use in order to encompass some individuals who identify towards masculine in the gender spectrum. Transmasculine individuals are a less-often recognized identity in the taxonomy of the FTM (female-to-male) community, yet appear to be as commonplace as any other contemporary self-identified individual.

Many transmasculine individuals, but not all, consider themselves to be *men*; however, there are also those who do not self-identify as *men* and choose instead to use a different term such as *genderqueer, gender variant, gender-fluid* or other to define themselves. One additional term worth noting that is similar in nature is that of *masculine-of-center*, used by various organizations such as Butch Voices and The Brown Boi Project, as well as many individuals.

There are, too, those who live as women, yet consider themselves *transmasculine*; the term *transmasculine* can include those who identify as *trans butch, butch boi, masculine of center*, and *stud*, to name a few. These masculine-identified women may well identify as *women*, yet the questioning of one's gender identity is not uncommon for them, and many have felt uncomfortable with being seen as girls/women. Some of these individuals waver between transitioning or not, simply because they have found a profound sense of camaraderie and solidarity in the lesbian community.

As a noun or an adjective, *butch* is a term that denotes masculine identity and/or behavior, and frequently defines a social role. It came to be popular in lesbian culture decades ago, although the politics around the term have gone through various shifts through the last few decades and, because of this, comes into passionate feminist and lesbian discourse often enough.

"*Transbutch* signifies a gendered embodiment that is both butch and trans, not tied to any singular definition of butch or trans but rather falling somewhere in between….The category of transbutch is a response to the hostility and misunderstanding displayed by some butches and lesbians toward transmen" ((Manion, 2014, p. 230).

Another author writes "Transbutches embrace aspects of masculinity without denouncing their social affiliation with an oppressed group of people who were predominantly raised and socialized as girls…. While butches or even transbutches might not identify as transgendered [sic], they are not cisgendered [sic] either (Manion, 2014, p. 231).

This next paragraph is one I wish to emphasize because it has been observed within the trans male communities that many consider the term *butch*, even when used with the clarifier of *trans*, is considered to mean *female* in the transmasculine arena and therefore does not belong in the trans *male* community. As a response to this line of thought, Manion continued to assert,

Transbutches relate to transmen and embrace their status as gender outlaws. Both share many of the following: identifying as more masculine than androgynous, taking pleasure from passing as male, assuming a male sexual identity, and rejecting the notion that biology is destiny…. As more transmen embrace top surgery and share powerful stories of pleasure and relief, butches are following their lead….in a group of transmen, the transbutch may or may not be accepted as a peer (2014, p. 231).

Transmasculine Identities Who Embrace Herstory

The title of this book was met with mixed, and even somewhat volatile emotion from members of the transmale/FTM community. Some understood immediately the context and accepted it as a reality for themselves, while others vehemently objected to the use of the word *herstory* rather than *history*. "I have always been a man, and I have *his*-tory, not *her*-story" was a common, and nicer than others, exclamation.

I acknowledge the men who do not claim *herstory* and I hope to convey my validation and recognition of your *history*. I also wish to make it very clear to Readers who may be just learning about the transmale/FTM community *that all transmen are not and may never have been lesbians*, and the larger portion of them do not embrace the term *herstory*. Again, this book is specifically for and about those who are comfortable with the term, and it is up to them in their stories to clarify how it relates to them or how it does not relate if they so choose; and how they prefer to be identified in their gender, their sexuality or their feminist perspectives.

As you read through the remaining chapters, you'll find in Part II the stories of men who spent a good portion of their lives as female and socialized in the female role. Some have emerged from the Lesbian community and a strong background in Feminist activity; while others were less vocal and active in mainstream Feminist movements, but very active in Lesbian activism, and others from all points in-between. Some lived among lesbians and were involved in lesbian relationships, yet never identified as one, but instead thought of themselves as men. There are those, too, just as commonly, who lived a typical heterosexual life, even marrying and having children; some of these individuals embarked on their identity journeys only to discover they were now able to claim the sexual identity of *gay male,* or just as commonly, a *heterosexual male.*

These men recognize their emergence into this world as designated females who lived in the social construction of that gender for a number of years. Some of them identified as female until such time that they found uncomfortableness in doing so and began exploring their masculine identities. Others assert there was an early onset of discomfort with their imposed social status, consciously identifying with the male gender as soon as they were mentally and emotionally old enough to do so.

There is no right or wrong to any one way of self-identification, although there is a sufficient amount of dissention about this fact within the community. Hansbury (2005) stresses the principle that individuality among people is located "in how each person interprets his or her own identity—how he or she perceives himself or herself, and how he or she wishes to be perceived by others" (p. 245).

I welcome you to continue reading, where you will find not only a more in-depth look at the deeper meaning of and the intersectionality of *gender, transgender, lesbianism* and *feminist thought,* but also stories shared by a variety of transmasculine identities with an assortment of backgrounds. There are diverse approaches regarding gender and transgender terminology, as well as various modalities of identities, sexualities, and orientation.

While you as the Reader may not agree or even understand some facets of the material or the lives of these individuals, I urge you to remember that these are individuals in the trans community as well as human beings in our society; their *herstories* are each being claimed and embraced by those who share them with you. Many of the men who embrace *herstory* have been silenced (one could even say they were still "closeted") due to the lack of understanding and acceptance within the FTM community, *perhaps even discriminated against within their social groups.*

This book provides them the opportunity to speak up and speak out about their experiences, and at the same time becomes an extraordinary opportunity for each of us to learn.

2

An Abundance of Gender

Rules for gender are associated with privileges and punishments as part of a system that privileges certain groups of people and oppresses others....privilege exists when one group has something of value that is denied to others simply because of the groups they belong to, rather than because of anything they've done or failed to do (Rands, 2009, p. 422).

In order to fully understand the background as well as the diversity of the transmasculine identities I am focusing on with this book, it is important to start with the basics—the very foundation of what is *male* and *female*, *men* and *women*, *masculine* and *feminine*. In one word, it all comes down to *gender*. This chapter is meant to take you further in the exploration of gender than the brief introduction found in Chapter 1, and as a stepping stone for later chapters.

Understanding gender is the key to comprehending the complexities that exist for some transmasculine identities, especially for those who discovered or developed their masculine identity while within the feminist and/or lesbian communities, as well as aiding in the understanding and significance of feminist thought by these individuals. It is this context where many have claimed their history, and for those especially who came from or learned from the second wave of feminism, their *herstory*. I'll talk more about transmasculine individuals and feminist thought in later chapters. For now, the focus is on the wonderful world of gender.

Biology vs. Social Constructs

The distinction between sex and gender has been noted by not only sociologists, feminists, gender scholars, transgender individuals, and others, it is also being recognized by various organizations and governmental entities around the world, each with their assorted but all too similar descriptions which help define where the separation between the two must exist. Many, however, still believe they are one and the same. Devor pointed this out in 1989, "Sex is believed to so strongly determine gender that these two classifications are commonly conflated to the extent the terms are used interchangeably" (p. 46). Some individuals have the contemporary understanding that sex and gender are distinctly different, and when asked to describe the difference, many would agree with Oakley's definition, "'Sex' is a word that refers to the biological differences between male and female: the visible difference in genitalia, the related difference in procreative function. 'Gender' however is a matter of culture: it refers to the social classification into 'masculine' and 'feminine'" (1985, pp. 21-22). This does not, however, account for that which is neither 'masculine' nor 'feminine'. We have the need for additional explanation.

The World Health Organization maintains that "Gender refers to the socially constructed characteristics of women and men – such as the norms, roles and relationships that exist between them," but they also go further by emphasizing that *It is also important to recognize identities that do not fit into the binary male or female sex categories*" ("Gender", 2015, p. 1). Now we are presented with the question, how does one identify with a gender that is not male or female? So we continue to seek answers to this growing dilemma called 'gender.'

Knowing what we do regarding the numerous variations of biological sex, how does one define 'gender' *except* through a socially constructed view of it? It has been long-standing that in knowing a baby's sex, one can then apply gender. But what exactly is 'gender' and how or why do we *apply* it? According to Oakley, it's both 'masculine' and 'feminine', yet there are those who do not appear to be in either specific category, those who have an *androgynous* presentation.

As a child, there is no incongruence or body dysphoria until confronted with the socially acceptable image society has placed upon their sex. Once this happens there can be shame, disgust, ridicule and discouragement from presenting as their true gender (Brown, 2015, pp. 27-28). People in society generally base their beliefs on the binary gender system;

so when they see someone who does not conform to their ideas or stereotyped beliefs of what they perceive as male or female, they react with fear and/or anger. Stereotypes "may contain some elements of truth....but they also fail to recognize individual differences and overlap between groups" (Best, 2003, p. 11).

Assigned at Birth

As we continue to seek answers, we realize that we need to understand more about biological sex and how it may or may not have an influence on gender. It is widely becoming understood that there are far more than just two sexes—man and woman—but rather there are estimates of up to 1 in 2,000 individuals who are born intersex ("How Common Is Intersex?", n.d.). This adds a variety of at least 70 more variations of biological sex (Haynes, 2001). This undisputedly and unequivocally dispels the idea of a simple, binary two sexes. There can be no argument or debate; it simply is scientific and proven.

With a physical inspection upon birth, a child is assigned a sex—either male or female—entirely dependent upon the visual inspection of its genitals. More often than not, however, different variations of intersex don't immediately present and are discovered later, sometimes after many years of having lived in the sex one was assigned at birth. As well, when there are physical signs of something other than what society determines as fully male or fully female, the physician or parents will make a decision for the child as to which binary sex they want it to be, or which they determine would be best for the child, and surgical intervention occurs. Creighton (2001, para. 7) wrote about this, stating "Clinicians aim to choose the gender that carries the best prognosis for reproductive and sexual function and for which the genitalia and physical appearance can be made to look most normal. It is thought this will ensure a stable gender identity."

However, there is grievous error in this statement. Clinicians are not choosing 'gender', they are choosing 'sex'. They are choosing *solely* on the basis of reproductive and sexual function, and which would appear more 'normal', which is, of course, subjective. There is also no way anyone can *ensure* any kind of 'stable' *gender identity*. In many cases, this crucial decision made without the child's consent is often found to be a significant mistake as the child begins to mature. Once the surgically altered child matures and their secondary sex characteristics (breasts, body hair, et cetera) appear, they are not always congruent with the choice made years earlier. Now we are presented with an individual who has been defined, raised and presented socially as one gender, yet now they display the physical characteristics and presentation of a different gender.

How Being Trans Challenges Gender

There are people whose physical bodies and the assigned sex they were given at birth do not match their inner personal gender identity. These are people who are *gender variant, transgender or transsexual*, as well as a myriad of other self-identifying terms. *Transgender* or *gender-variant* individuals experience their gender differently than people who are *cisgender*. *Cisgender* is a term for people who are not *transgender*. As Susan Stryker (2008, p.22) states, "the prefix *cis-* means 'on the same side as' (that is, the opposite of *trans*)." The incongruities of a mismatched *sex* and *gender* are often felt by these individuals prior to school age; but there are also many who don't begin experiencing the discomfort until much later in life.

Imagine what happens to individuals who have been raised in the *gender role* of a chosen or assigned sex. Author Julia T. Wood says "What gender means and how we express it depend on a society's values, beliefs and preferred ways of collective life" (Wood, 2012, p. 23). With society's views and beliefs, we subject ourselves and all newborns to certain social cues that define gender. "The child will be given certain colors of clothing, certain types of toys and be treated differently depending on his or her sex while growing up. Behavior and attitudes will be displayed and defined by parents, siblings, peers, teachers and eventually employers" (Brown, 2015, p. 59).

A child does not *automatically* know gender or gender roles. The child watches and learns, because children model behaviors; these behaviors are performed by those already enmeshed in their socially-prescribed gender roles. "Their teachers are many, ranging from parents, siblings, and peers to television, popular music, and magazines. Not only are these messages ubiquitous and multivariate, but they are constantly reinforced through the threat of ridicule, humiliation, and physical violence should an individual fail to abide by them" (Schifter & Madrigal, 2000, p.95). As stated in Chapter 1, a child *due to these social cues*, generally understands its gender and the roles before the age of five.

So What Exactly IS Gender?

Now we can get to the crux of what gender *is*, and how it is defined, presented or declared, and there is no simpler way of defining it than how Kate Bornstein managed to sum it up in one short paragraph of what could take volumes to explain any better:

> Instead of saying that all gender is this or all gender is that, let's recognize that the word gender has scores of meaning built into it. It's an amalgamation of bodies, identities, and life experiences, subconscious urges, sensations, and behaviors, some of which develop organically, and others which are shaped by language and culture. Instead of saying that gender is any one single thing, let's start describing it as a holistic experience. (Bornstein & Bergman, 2010, p. 87).

It's really that simple. *Gender is whatever we choose it to be.*

※◇※

The Complexity of Lesbian Gender

Now that we have a fairly good grasp on the fact that gender is fluid and changeable and in no way itself solid, I want to talk a little about lesbians and gender, with the assortment of masculinity and femininity involved. Not all transmasculine individuals were lesbian-identified at any time, but since many do come from this background, it is important to look at it closer in order to understand the dynamics and subtleties of some transmasculine individuals.

Levitt & Hiestand acknowledged the complications that lesbian gender brought up, by examining the genders of "butch" and "femme". They wrote of women in the 1940s and 1950s who participated in the lesbian community by adopting a butch or femme appearance and interactional style, because "The ability to pass offered butch women opportunities for employment, a safety from harassment, as well as an identity within the lesbian community" (2004, p. 605). They also state that femme women exaggerated the signs of traditional femininity, while the style of butch women was read as masculine by heterosexuals. By the 1970s with the feminist movement going on at that time, however, the feminist community, both heterosexual and lesbians alike began viewing "the butch/femme dynamics as mimicking the patriarchal relationships that they were challenging....butches were accused of claiming male privilege" (Levitt & Hiestand, 2004, p. 606) and lesbians began to take on a more androgynous appearance through the 1970s. By the 1980s, the butch/femme culture began to reappear (Faderman, 1991).

✠✠✠

The focus of this book is on the diversity of genders and sexualities—there are far too many combinations to list. Yet again, we cannot overlook the individuals who embrace an identity or set of identities that make others uncomfortable. I am bringing up this next identity combination, because it seems to be troublesome for so many, yet is not at all uncommon among the transmasculine community. I have known several of these people over the years, and you'll even meet more than one in this book as you continue reading.

Many of us question how a lesbian can claim a transmasculine identity, or looking at it in reverse, how a transmasculine identity could also identify as a lesbian, which is, in effect, blurring the lines of gender. It is important to understand, as I wrote in Chapter 1, (remember the story of Lee?) some transmasculine individuals identify as transgender, while still socially identifying as lesbian. Both transgender and cisgender individuals seem to find this distressing. Think about the individual faced now with lesbians who claim that if a female-bodied person identifies as a man, even going so far as to surgically modify their body, then they are no longer a lesbian, and similarly faced with those in the transgender community, especially those who are "binary," who make the same claim. This individual now experiences discrimination within the same communities who have fought against discrimination against themselves.

Where does this leave the self-identifying transmasculine individual who has had breast reconstruction surgery or uses male hormones, and uses male pronouns and yet is still lesbian-identified? The social ramifications of a medically-altered transmasculine lesbian has now became an outcast from both communities, and somehow becomes "lesser than" in either category. Ideas about these individuals become *convoluted and discriminating*. As an example, when lesbians were asked for thoughts about lesbians who transition to male, one participant wrote:

> *They are still lesbian women as transition changes outwards gender presentation not sex....it bothers me that female homosexuals pretend to be heterosexual men....I won't call them he or play along*

with their delusions anymore then I would call a woman with an eating [dis]order fat because she sees herself that way....The only groups I would exclude them from are those they claim to no longer be part of because lesbian women don't need women who are not proud lesbian women among us. Nor do I believe they belong among men, but it's not like they will be oppressing heterosexual men by invading their spaces where if outed they will still be treated as the females they are. (Anonymous, 37, Lesbian)

There are some transmen who seem to have similar discriminating thought-patterns, as this anonymous survey participant wrote:

I hate when transmen say that they're a lesbian...that just contra-dicts everything we've been fighting for and sets a horrible example to those who may not understand what being trans is like. Lesbian is love between two women/female identifying people. Not two vagina people. That's like saying you are what your body is in terms of sexuality which is disgusting because they're basically saying "welp, you are what your body is so if u have a vagina u must be female so u gotta be a lesbian if you love a female." Transmasculine people/trans men cannot be lesbians unless they're lying about ei-ther their gender or sexuality. (Transman/FTM, 48, Same-gender loving,)

Sadly, neither of these two survey participants were alone in their per-spectives. Although the greater majority of lesbian participants were sur-prisingly accepting of this situation of transmen claiming a lesbian iden-tity, fewer trans individuals (those who identified as either male, trans-man or FTM) were as tolerant or open-minded to the idea.

Loree Cook-Daniels (1999) asks a thought-provoking question which encourages deep consideration about this issue,

Why is it that masculinity in a body whose owner says she is female feels so different to us when the owner of that body says he is male? When those bodies are one in the same, what, precisely, do we perceive as having changed? ....What does it mean about any of our political analyses when we see members of "us" become mem-bers of "them"? Is it possible that we've outgrown our conception that "male" and "female," "lesbian" and "straight" are separate, unbridgeable categories? Is it possible we have been way too simplistic about who is for us and who is against us? (p. 1-2).

The truth is, just as there are an immeasurable number of genders and gender identifications, there are also equally as many sexual identifications, and all can be the proverbial "mix and match" when it comes to a *personal*—not social—decision about who we are. No one identification is any more—or less—valid than any other, and it is not up to society (including the trans and LGB communities) to define any individual, or discriminate because that individual doesn't seem to "conform" to their limited vision of what is "normal" for their community.

Trans and gender-nonconforming individuals have been "othered" by mainstream society, why must they endure this among the very communities of which they are a part. Chapter 3 will expand on transmasculinity, and come back to the discussion on lesbian identity, while Chapter 5 is going revisit all of the ideas presented in order to facilitate an awareness of intergroup discrimination and concerns. The topic of lesbian identity is important to recognize in relation to transmasculinity; without this understanding, we are at risk of a community divided rather than united. With gender non-conforming, genderqueer and non-binary transmasculine individuals being recognized as part of the *transgender umbrella,* they deserve the same validation and support that self-identified binary trans men demand.

3

The Social Construct of
Transmasculine Identities

There is no one pattern of masculinity that is found everywhere. Different cultures and different periods of history, construct masculinity differently.... Equally important, more than one kind of masculinity can be found within a given cultural setting....Masculinities do not exist prior to social behavior, either as bodily states or as fixed personalities. Rather, masculinities come into existence as people act. They are accomplished in everyday conduct or organizational life, as configurations of social practice (Connell, 1996, pp. 208, 210).

Now that we've established a sort of "groundwork" for understanding gender and sexuality, it is time to move on to explore the masculine side of the gender spectrum, specifically *transmasculinity*, in more depth. To do so means to understand what *masculinity* entails. A simplistic, and inadequate, definition is given in a document published by the U.S. Department of Health and Human Services, which states, "Although no one set of behaviors or traits defines masculinity, certain characteristics or expectations are associated with masculinity in a broad range of cultural contexts and across different age groups" (SAMHSA, 2013, para. 15). As you can see, we are still left with wondering what these characteristics or expectations might be, and is our own definition of masculinity accurate, or culturally and socially constructed and perhaps malleable?

The stereotypical roles that define men within a culture are referred to as "masculinity ideologies" (Good et al., 1994). These ideologies are systems of beliefs, values or ideas within a social group, and are many times thought to be truth. When speaking of masculinity ideologies, we are forced to remember the socially constructed ideas of gender, a concept explained in Chapter 1. These ideologies affect how men think and feel about themselves and other men, and can be a source of pride, as well as a position of power and privilege.

Author Jamison Green (2005) asked a group of transmen and cisgender men a set of six questions about their own ideas of masculinity. The question that gave the greatest difference in responses was "What does it mean to be masculine or to have masculinity?" For transmen, masculinity meant power and privilege; but for the cisgender men, masculinity meant having a "particular psychic destiny that is opposite and complimentary to that of femininity" (p. 297). Green goes on to give his conclusion about what he learned about masculinity in this particular group through his set of questions and the diverse array of answers:

> Masculinity is a socially negotiable quality that is understood through agreed-on symbols (such as the body and its secondary sex characteristics) and signals (such as clothing, behaviors, occupations, speech patterns, etc., understood within a given cultural context) that together inform other people in that context concerning the individual person's status in a given group (p. 297).

Quite a mouthful, isn't it? I will try to break it down even more, then examine just how diverse masculinity really is.

Many academics and authors have studied and written on masculinity as it relates to FTMs; and, like gender and sexuality, it is in the proverbial "eye of the beholder." There is no one right way to be, do, or portray masculinity. Masculinity is not confined to male-bodied individuals, as I've mentioned briefly earlier in this book. Female masculinity is no less masculine if we are using the definition of masculinity as a collection of behaviors, actions, qualities, and social characteristics (Forshee, 2006). Green talks about masculinity and the conferred privilege on a man, but at the same time it is also the target of ridicule meant to devalue men. He realized his own masculinity was not what was being questioned, it was the maleness of his perceived male body: he found that masculinity in a female body causes a different set of reactions than masculinity in a male body, something for which he had not been prepared. He says of the experience "I reflected on all the years I had thought my masculinity was the problem for my female body, and came to understand, more concretely than before, that it was my female body that had been the problem for my masculinity" (2004, p. 36).

Recall the question Loree Cook-Daniels asked that I referred to in Chapter 2, why masculinity in a body who identifies as female and that of one who identifies as male feels different to us? I will try to break it down, then, and see if there is truly a difference, or if it is a matter of individual perception.

⬦⬦⬦

Is There a Difference Between Male and Female Masculinity?

When we think of female-bodied individuals who exhibit masculine appearance or behaviors, it is not always considered non-normative. Female children with expressions of masculinity [tomboys, for example] are not only accepted: they are often viewed positively (Safir, Rosenmann, & Kloner, 2003). Once these children get older, however, society's perceptions begin to change. In time, this person presenting themselves against the social norm becomes something "other", often perceived as lesbian, or as a man-hater, or in the case of a professional, they are perceived as aggressive and bossy.

Thinking about masculinity being a behavior—consider how a butch woman might be seen as behaving badly, yet it would not be attributed to her sex or gender, or her self-identification, or even her history. If an FTM, however, exhibits the same behaviors, these behaviors are likely to be labeled "male" and be attributed to gender or identification or history. Consider, too, what happens when someone whose gender identity is not consistent, but shaped by "passing" as male or female in different contexts, such as perhaps an androgynous-appearing butch, who could be lesbian. Or FTM. Or both. Halberstam explores how the concept of "becoming" then relates to someone whose gender identity is not consistent, shaped by "passing" as male or female in different contexts. For example, what of the butch who in some instances passes as male and others as female, but presents a gender that is neither in alignment with women or man? Halberstam also asserts that "masculinity must not and cannot and should not reduce down to the male body and its effects" (1998b, p. 2, 22).

It should be obvious now that masculinity is a social construct, and those who were born female-bodied experience this masculinity differently according to the time and setting; in other words, depending on the perceptions of the individuals around him or her. Hansbury (2005) talks about this "middle" place, and how it is occupied by every transmasculine person, and underneath the beard or the three-piece suit, and whether or not they have had surgery or hormones, the individual remains "beyond the binary." He writes of this dichotomy of gender and perception (repeated here from Chapter 1 because of its importance in understanding self-identification), "Someone may identify as a Transsexual Man yet still maintain his breasts and forgo testosterone. Another may choose to undergo a mastectomy, take low-dosage testosterone, and identify as a Passing Woman" (p. 245). I believe we must also recognize that, as Halberstam states, "some bodies are never at home, some bodies cannot simply cross from A to B, some bodies recognize and live with the inherent instability of identity" (1998b, p. 164).

So where does the line between female masculinity and male masculinity fall when it is presented by a trans individual? As well, we cannot leave out some butch women, those who can be considered part of the trans community, because "they fall outside of traditional male and female categories....Butch women....traverse the boundaries of gender" (Halberstam, 1998b, p. 620). Zimman says that transmasculinity "is not a special—or single—type of masculinity" (2014, p. 197), but rather it is enacted by people with transgender identities.

There is no line, there are only societal perceptions. It is up to each individual to define their own identity and their own version of what masculinity means to them. There are no absolutes when it comes to transmasculinity. It is a self-identification that relates in some way to masculinity, but that relation is diverse as gender and sexuality. Stephen Whittle (2000) asked "Am I a man or a woman or something else entirely? ....Gender is thus centrally concerned with who one considers oneself to be, not how one appears to others" (p. 7).

❦❦❦

When asked for personal definitions of masculinity, an acquaintance in a group I belong to wrote:

> *I've been told that men aren't supposed to give a shit about what others say because they're sure of themselves and other things. These*

societal ideas of masculinity are so ingrained in me now I can't find my own definitions of masculinity. I know that I personally do give a shit so I don't fit that one! Clearly, transmen are redefining what it is to be masculine then. I do think male and female masculinity is different to a degree only because of my own experiences. When I was a butch I thought if I just acted as macho as possible then I wouldn't have to transition. Boy, was I wrong! Nothing I did was ever masculine enough. When I transitioned and was seen as male I was then able to tone down some of that stereotypical macho behavior. (Shannon, Early 40's, Transman)

Another individual considered the concept, and also had trouble defining it personally. He wrote,

I'm still figuring that out. This stuff is all so blurred for me. I've had my gender questioned since I was very young (around 8 or 9) and because I'm pre T, I still do. There are many aspects of traditional masculinity that I want no part of (violence, being uncaring, etc.). I often feel like a stereotypical gay male and love "camp." A friend suggested that this was a safe way for me to allow my femininity to show. Maybe they're right and maybe they're not. Since I'm really still just coming out socially as a trans guy, this concept of masculinity and femininity is very fuzzy. The one thing I do know is that when my new legal name is used or I'm called "he/him/Sir", it feels so right.

I feel like the extremes of it that our culture perpetuate are social constructs that can limit us in so many ways. They are the extremes that tell men they can't cry, be soft. They are the same things that discourage women from going into male dominated fields and value women's lives as less than men. I guess maybe that's patriarchy. But being masculine is as natural to me as having blue eyes, and now, gray hair. My masculinity doesn't look like a lot of people's traditional ideas of masculinity.

My wife asked me recently (as I've socially transitioned everywhere in the last few weeks) if I will still like things like getting pedicures, watching sappy movies and vaginal penetration. The answer is yes. There is a lot of fluctuation in my being. I guess I'm figuring out as I get older that there is a lot more fluctuation in this gender stuff than I ever thought there was. And personally, I love it. (Casey, 51, Non-binary FTM)

Not everyone "loves it," however. There are those who were more masculine-identified and lived as lesbians, then pursued medical transition only to discover that being masculine-identified as a man was not working for them. They lost friends in the lesbian community, which is a profound loss for many trans men, so they proceeded to detransition, losing friends in the trans community. Pay attention to the last three words of this story:

> I am considered societally within the transgender 'umbrella' - my birth certificate says F, my passport says M, my body is ambiguous. But I reject trans ideology as it applies to me and I do not want to consider myself 'transgender.' I was born a woman, lived as a lesbian, then lived as a trans man. I took testosterone for 2.5 years and have had bilateral mastectomy. I am identified as transmasculine, but I do not identify myself as transmasculine. I reject the idea of 'trans' now. I lost friends both times. I don't have any more than one friend from before transition, but on detransition, none of my trans-identified friends talked to me either. Nobody wants it. (Anonymous, 22, Trans-sexed, detransitioned woman, lesbian)

How sad is this? A person on a journey of self-discovery, but rejected by the very communities that should understand gender and sexual diversity more than the rest of society. The rejection from lesbians because self-identification was male, then rejection from the trans community because self-identification was female. Devor maintained "there is much overlap between the lesbian, gay, bisexual, and queer communities and trans communities….We engage in social and legal wrangling to decide what actually counts to qualify one to be able to legitimately claim membership in a particular sex category" (2002, p. 5, 7). One can substitute the word "gender" in place of 'sex' as well, and there are constant battles within the community of who is or is not "trans enough," who is "really trans," and so forth (a subject I will touch on briefly in Chapter 6).

Back to the original question, is there a difference between male and female masculinity? I believe there is—but only in the eyes of the beholder, which is merely individual perception influenced by socially constructed ideas. If masculinity is indeed a set of behaviors and appearance, then it can be applicable to all genders, regardless of biological sex, personal identification, or social perception. I personally don't "feel" masculine (or feminine) with general society's perception of what these two words might mean. They are socially constructed and are variable. They are not binary or biological like the words *male* and *female*. They are fluid and expressed by all genders to varying degrees. I lean towards "being" a binary trans man, but I acknowledge my social upbringing as female and embrace it. I do not consider myself non-binary, I am a (trans) man, but a man with both masculine and feminine traits. I cannot shun the first part of my life, it made me the strong person I feel I am today. If that is masculine, then fine, and if it is remnants of femaleness, so be it. You can read the Preface if you skipped it to know more about me.

Transmasculine and Lesbian?

Why not? With all you have read so far, is there any doubt that a person could identify as both? Remember my friend Lee from Chapter 1 who identified as a transgender man, yet lived socially as a lesbian? As I wrote in the first two chapters, there are, indeed, individuals who consider themselves to be both a transgender man and a lesbian. Why is this important to the understanding transmasculinity? Because people have preconceived ideas about not only gender with its masculine and feminine traits, they also have their ideas about sexuality and the terms used to describe both identification and orientation. Dr. Jillian T. Weiss asserts "Being a woman who considers herself transgender does not mean abandoning one's identity as a lesbian and taking on an FTM identity" (p. 205). In the same token, a female-to-male individual can identify as a man, and continue to identify as a lesbian. I believe there are as many self-definitions and identifications as there are people on this planet. It is not our job to agree or disagree with them, it is up to us to respect them.

In a 2015-2016 informal questionnaire in which I asked how transmasculine individuals identified both in past gender and sexuality as well as current gender and sexuality, the answers were all over the scale. Here are a few of the responses of those who identified as lesbian prior to identifying as transgender, and their thoughts on the continued use of the identification of lesbian while being somewhere on the masculine side of the gender spectrum.

> *I am a non-binary transman. Usually to cut out the confusion I tell*
> *people I am queer but at my core I identify as a lesbian despite my*

trans identity. I think of myself as a man but not male and that the current way we define sexuality is painfully narrow. We should open up terns like gay and lesbian to have the potential of accepting non binary individuals. (Anonymous, 20, transgender, lesbian)

I am not heterosexual because I am not a binary male. I am a lesbian non-binary man. I identify as a man but not male, I use the term lesbian because I feel that I occupy a space between transmasculine and binary man and lesbian is not a purely female term. (Anonymous, non-binary man, 22, lesbian)

One individual had a lot to say about this:

I tried to abandon the idea of myself as a lesbian because that seemed to be what the trans community required of FTMs and trans men. If you're a man then you can't be a woman, and you have to be a woman to be a lesbian, right? But I still felt like a lesbian, and in a way, I felt like a woman, too. Finally I decided that it didn't matter what other people thought of it, I had to reclaim the part of myself that felt like a lesbian, for me. I feel so much better since I did that.

I think being trans is inherently "both" or "between." Some people don't like that, and really do wish they could just have been born the other sex. However, I don't think we're all like that. I think some of us are less resistant to the idea of being both or a mix. However, you don't see that put forth as "The Narrative"; you more often see people rejecting everything associated with their birth sex. I think, although I can't know, that the internal experiences of many people who identify as genderqueer vs. experiences of those identify as "binary' trans people or "regular" MTF/FTM might not be so divergent as we think. I suspect that "genderqueer' arose to fill a need for people who were trying to voice the duality of being trans and tell a story that they didn't see being told.

When I first started becoming involved in the trans community online, the impression I got was that "genderqueer" was someone who was just as trans as a binary trans person, their goal was just different. Their "target gender" didn't coincide exactly with male or female, but they felt dysphoria and at least some of them wanted to transition. Since then, I have noticed the category of genderqueer opening up to include gender-conforming people who seem to have a much "softer" form of whatever it is we have that makes us trans. Some of them are much closer to "cis," but for whatever reason, they feel the need to name something that they are experiencing.

In a way, I think "genderqueer" is a way of naming the hazy area between "cis" and "trans". I think a lot of LGB people like genderqueer because it gives them a way to name what they have in common with trans people due to being gender non-conforming. I think a lot of LGB people are "soft trans," and we share some of the same feelings, but theirs might not be as severe. I think especially for transmasculine people who are also lesbians (or used to be lesbians), it allows them to claim their femaleness and their connection to (other) women, while acknowledging the trans male part of themselves. (Anonymous, 28, non-binary, lesbian)

Not all trans men agree on using the term lesbian to describe a masculine identity, in fact the numbers are quite low, and the reactions to the thought of it are not always polite. *This does not make this embodiment any less valid,* however. In an informal survey, 91 trans men of all ages answered a question on how they felt about any trans man who identified as a lesbian. Forty-seven of them felt that it is up to the individual, but thirty were quite adamant that this was unacceptable, seven were unsure or had not thought about it, and seven identified as lesbian.

One of them takes it personally in a negative way when a trans man identifies as a lesbian (for what reason was unexplained), yet is open-minded in considering the overall concept and wrote the following thoughts for us:

Transmasculine people in the broader sense don't bother me at all; the category of "butch" has always included people who would now be described as "transmasculine," and I've known older butches who were active in the lesbian scene in the 60s and 70s who used male names, male pronouns, described themselves as having wives etc. The separation between "transmasculine person" and "lesbian" is a relatively recent and artificial one.

I even understand why some trans men consider themselves lesbians as well - many trans men are seen that way on a daily basis, either because they're read visually as women, because they can't access legal gender change and so are affected by laws (marriage, etc.) that affect lesbians, or because when people know they're trans

> *they're promptly identified as lesbians ... I can see how claiming "lesbian" could be an act of defiance and self-affirmation in these situations, uncomfortable as it makes me myself.*
>
> *This is really down to the individual....sexual identity is complicated and I think "transmasculine" accommodates a wider range that I think could include "lesbian" as a sexual identity if that's what the individual prefers....I think whatever level of comfort the individual is at with their identification is correct for them at this stage of their development.* (Anonymous, Man/Male, 35, Gay)

Forshee (2008) says that it is important to make a distinction between an FTM gender identity and a lesbian sexual identity, they have commonalities such as gender expression, but not all those who transition from female to male take on a heterosexual identity, nor does female masculinity always provoke a transition into a male body. Jamison Green (2005) puts it all into perspective, "Trans or nontrans, when individuals realize that they can give up the struggle of trying to prove who they are, or how butch they are, or how male, or how masculine, they can realize that whatever qualities of character they have, they are all part of the package" (p. 298-299).

⬥⬥⬥

Terminology Tidbits

There are two schools of thought on transgender people and their sexual orientations. In order to put these two views into perspective, consider a transgender man who has socially transitioned to living as a male and identifying as such. In the early days, when the Standards of Care (WPATH) dictated a trans person was to successfully live as the "opposite" gender for a year or more, undergo a physical, medical transition with hormones and surgery, then live in a typically heterosexual social role and be attracted only to the newly "opposite" sex, in this case, females. Many considered these men to be "homosexual", because their biology was female and their sexual interests were towards females—an essentialist view. This was not a comfortable situation for those trans men who were attracted to men, or were bisexual. Many also believed that because they were a man, they could not be homosexual if they were attracted to women, as men who love women are heterosexual.

This binary rigid idea was soon replaced by social constructionism, the belief that once this person had begun living in a male role, his sexual orientation was more fluid, and because he was a man, he was no longer considered homosexual if his sexual interest and/or orientation was towards women. Constructionism and Queer Theory opened the door to other possibilities. Trans men (and women) could live authentically as the man or woman they are, with the freedom to be attracted to and love any or all genders, and claim any identity terminology that was comfortable for them personally, whether straight, gay, lesbian, bisexual, or pansexual, among a plethora of others.

As the trans community advocates for autonomy and equality, terminology continues to transform. What once was accepted as fact is now challenged on a daily basis as identities and orientations surface and become the "norm." A large number of terms have emerged, developing over the past thirty to forty years, with most becoming fashionable in the new millennium. For some people, the older terms are 'antiquated' and should be eliminated altogether, while others have embraced certain older terminology for themselves, such as transsexual, and are hesitant, if not fully against, altering their views. There are still those who refuse to acknowledge and embrace the term "queer" to describe themselves, as it is a word that only became popular in the 1990s. For decades, it was a slur against lesbians and gay men, but the community began to embrace it for themselves, adding "Q" to the LGBTQ acronym (which was only after struggles to add first the "B" and finally the "T"). Today the popular acronym includes many more letters, and "Queer" has evolved to meaning much more than just sexuality, it is now popular in terms of gender, such as in "Genderqueer."

It all comes back to self-identification, however, with the autonomy and ability to embrace any term one feels comfortable using. Because someone chooses what others might consider an antiquated or even questionable term, it should not invalidate them as a person, or in any way negate their trans-ness. To debate the semantics of a term that any one individual has chosen for themselves because of your perception of their gender, gender expression or their sexuality is to, essentially, dismiss their right to be themselves. This goes against all for which the trans community has been advocating in their right to self-expression and self-identification.

❈❈❈

A Herstory of Transmasculine Identities

Masculinity and Transmasculinity

If masculinity is socially defined, can be demonstrated by men and women, and is perceived and derived from behaviors and appearances, then could it be that masculinity, as well as femininity, could blur the lines of gender? And, if so, could blurring and blending the lines of gender mean that all people in some way might exhibit *transmasculine* (or *transfeminine*) behavior or appearance? Or just gays, lesbians and bisexuals could do this? And, if just gays, lesbians and bisexuals, what does sexual orientation have to do with gender? In seeing "flamboyancy" in a man, he is automatically perceived to be "gay". In seeing a masculine woman, she is automatically perceived to be a lesbian. These statements are true both within the wider society as well as within the LGBT community. Yet gender presentation really has nothing to do with sexual orientation.

I have spent quite a bit of time asking these types of question in trans mens' groups on social media, (i.e. what is masculinity? What is transmasculinity? If appearance is a quantifier, then what do we perceive when seeing a trans man wearing makeup and is this different than seeing a cisgender man in makeup?) Thorough and well-thought out answers are difficult to come by, because most people answer not with their personal perception of what masculinity or transmasculinity is, but with rather generic answers, like "To each his own" or "There are too many labels, people should be allowed to express themselves in any way they want." I am not sure if this is due to their belief they are actually answering the questions, or maybe they really do not know, or could it be they are cautious in sharing their true feelings for fear of offending someone else? Then I have to wonder about, and this thought was inspired by a conversation with a different crowd and another question: Are trans men, in general, silent on some things because they were socialized as females, given that females are conditioned to stay silent because their opinions don't count? Could it be that they really don't know what they feel, because they have been told their feelings are invalid? Or could they be avoiding confrontation because it is easier?

As you can see, the questions can just get deeper, more complicated and even controversial. What it all boils down to, however, is that *transmasculine* is an identifier that *only* an individual can give to themselves, whether that person is male or female, whether there has been surgery or hormones, and whether or not that person dresses or acts masculine. Transmasculinity is a term reserved for those who claim it, and no other person has a right to try to define or redefine in order to make themselves more comfortable.

※※※

Trans men are redefining what it is to be masculine.

Not all trans men identify as transmasculine, and those who do may not agree on levels or types of masculinity. What is an undisputed fact, however, is that *trans men are redefining what it is to be masculine.* In doing so, they are also confronting and aiding in the role of Feminism in society, and, as well, societal perceptions of masculinity are expanding ever-so-slowly into a realization that both masculinity and femininity are social constructs, not something immutable or absolute. Transmasculinity challenges society to examine the deeper meaning of what it means to be a man or a woman, regardless of the physical body or gender expression.

4

The Intersection of Feminism and Transmasculinity

Author Note: I feel it is important to provide a brief synopsis of feminism in order to support the assertion that transmasculine identities, trans men in this case, are no less of a man because they choose not only to embrace their female pasts, and some may also affirm their *herstory* as a valid component of their lives. This also infers they are no less of a feminist simply because they embody masculinity. These men acknowledge the importance of the feminist values they support as well as the imposed social roles that challenged them, because these experiences have made them the person they are today.

From what has been shown in previous chapters, we can understand and agree that gender is reinforced constantly during our lifetimes. We can also acknowledge that gender identity and sexual identity are both fluid, and there is no one way or right way to personally identify in either capacity. Whether one chooses to use the term *trans,* or *transgender, transsexual, transmasculine,* or any other term to describe one's self, it is a personal choice; and whether one chooses to claim their sexual identity is lesbian or gay man or heterosexual or other, each and all are not only acceptable, but appropriate for them personally. Conformity to an explicit and conventional way of thought is only specific to those who agree with the thought and it is up to *no one* to state one way or another is more or less acceptable.

In Chapter 1, I wrote about a past partner of mine, Lee. I will repeat some of it here for you to keep in mind as you continue reading this chapter, because I think it is important to keep a personal perspective as you try to make sense of all that will be said here.

> Lee self-identified as a male as well as a transgender man…. she preferred people in her social life to refer to her with female pronouns….She lived socially as a lesbian…[and she] chose to speak of her own *herstory* as a transmasculine individual because of her self-identification as lesbian and as a feminist. This did not make her any less of a man, nor any greater of a woman.

Not at all feminine in appearance nor mannerisms, Lee would have fit right in with some of today's younger generation of transmasculine individuals– those on the masculine side of the gender spectrum who choose not to embrace the binaries of 'male' and 'female'. Perhaps 'queer' would be a word she would have used today, although in the early 1990s she was dead-set against it. She was very secure in her gender and sexual identities, and felt that being a man did not preclude her from using female pronouns or a feminist term for her story. A great many non-binary and queer individuals understand the combination of male/female and accept this without question, and some even self-identify much in the same way that Lee did, as you saw when you read their words in Chapter 3.

However, there are also many who would claim that she was really not a man if she was using female pronouns or embracing the female side of her. Their reasoning is that if Lee were a man, then *he* was never a female, *he* was always a man, and men cannot and do not relate to a female past. I maintain that in making this declarative statement, "No one is a man if they use female pronouns and embraces *herstory*" it is nothing short of the same type of closed-minded attitudes that we (the trans community) face in wider society against all things trans,

If you are someone in the category of advocating for rights of trans people to be equal and free of discrimination, I ask you to think deeply about the following questions as you continue to read this chapter, and perhaps take some time to reflect on your thoughts.

1. Who am I to say whether a person is more or less

trans, is or is not a man or a woman, or what pronouns they can or cannot use?

2. How does this make me any different than those in society that have created these rigid gender roles in the first place?

3. Is this not an example of inflexible thinking from a binary perspective?

4. If we are fighting for inclusion and the right to be heard and treated with respect, should we not show the same to those fighting beside us?

❈❈❈

Along with society-imposed gender roles there comes a power structure. One of the strongest determinants for the gender system is patriarchal hegemonic gender beliefs—male stereotypes, or in other words, *masculinities*, functioning as an aspect of a larger structure, (Connell, 2005), which proceed to perpetuate this system. So much so, in fact, that some women, or *femininities*, have co-opted this structure, creating benevolent sexist attitudes towards women who do not conform to stereotypical roles (Sibley, Overall & Duckett, 2007). Ridgeway and Correll assert that cultural beliefs about gender govern the entire gender system, and these beliefs have self-fulfilling effects on perceptions and behaviors which allow them to continue to persist even when facing social change (2004, p.527). These ideologies have existed for centuries, even thousands of years; every society, to some degree, assigns tasks on the basis of gender, and there is no society that places the status of women superior to men (Munroe & Munroe, 1975/1994). Anthropologic studies have confirmed that whether men were the hunters or the gatherers, or no matter what tasks they held, "they had greater status, prestige and material resources than women" (Jeanes, Knights & Martins, 2012, p. 213). Chapter 6 offers a greater focus on gender inequities.

It is no wonder that women over the years began protesting the inequities, and these women came to be known as *feminists*. From the early 1900s and Women's Suffrage to the Women's Liberation movement, Second- and Third-waves and beyond, women have challenged the male-dominated hegemonic control of society. "Simply put, feminism is a movement to end sexism, sexist exploitation, and oppression…. Practically, it is a definition which implies that all sexist thinking and action is the problem, whether those who perpetuate it are female or male, child or adult." (hooks, 2000, p. 1)

For those who wish to have a deeper understanding of what feminism really is, an even broader definition might be:

> Feminism is the advocacy of women's rights surrounding political, social, and economic equality to men. It is an effort to rid society of stereotyping, objectification, infringements of human rights, or gender, or sexuality-based oppression, and is active in areas such as domestic violence, reproductive rights, social justice, and in workplace issues such as equal pay, family medical leave, and sexual harassment and discrimination (Brown, 2016).

During the second-wave of feminism, the argument for sex and gender distinction existed, but there were those who believed there was a conflict between transgender identity and the feminist cause. This was partly due to Janice Raymond, author of *The Transsexual Empire*, who argued that genitalia permanently determine one's essential identity, and that trying to violate the divide between man and woman was impossible, unnatural and unhealthy. She claimed that only biological females can genuinely feel what occupying a woman's a body is like (Raymond, 1980). Second-wave feminists felt that trans people embraced traditional gender roles and stereotypes; by the third-wave of feminism, trans people were becoming more accepted, but only to an extent. Some, like Firestone (1970), believe that gender is totally undetermined by sex, thus helping pave the way for trans, non-binary and atypically gendered people to move ahead in their own fight for fair treatment and equality. Not all feminist-thinking people fully support trans men and women, but many do see the intersectionality and are inclusive in their fight to remove oppression and marginalization from all facets of society.

During the 1970s, feminists felt that the inclusion of lesbians would hinder their movement because "were considered to have distinct issues that would draw attention away from the issues of the heterosexual majority… [but] lesbian communities accused feminists of engaging in heterosexist and patriarchal lesbian baiting" (E. Green, 2006, p. 242). By the end of the decade, lesbianism was representative of feminism due to the liberation from male dependency.

Next, they encountered transgender people joining in the struggles for equality. Trans identities and inclusion within the feminist movement have historically been met with varying degrees of opposition. Because trans women are born biologically male, they are sometimes automatically seen as the enemy, while trans men have made a choice to "abandon" their femaleness in order to "join forces" and become the enemy (Halberstam, 1998b). Academic and trans activist Eli R. Green suggests that by including trans people in the feminist movement, it would force cisgender feminists to acknowledge "that 'woman' is not the only oppressed gender [and] it would force feminists to recognize gender-variant persons as *validly gendered*" (2006, p. 243). Green also mentions that cisgender women experience the privilege of being part of a legitimate social class—the class of "woman"—but that trans people are marginalized and are victims of violence strictly because of their gender-variance. It seems that this marginalization would be a cause for concern among feminists as something for which to rally, but there are those who see the trans community as outsiders.

Many feminists state emphatically that males cannot be feminist or even truly understand. Author bell hooks (2000) disagrees and argues, "Without males as allies in struggle feminist movement will not progress...A male who has divested of male privilege, who has embraced feminist politics, is a worthy comrade in struggle, in no way a threat to feminism, whereas a female who remains wedded to sexist thinking and behavior infiltrating feminist movement is a dangerous threat" (p. 12).

I recently witnessed a discussion thread on Facebook between a cisgender man and a small group of transwomen in a trans feminist group. He identified himself as a "trans ally" and was immediately attacked by these women who believed that a cisgender man could never be a trans ally or a feminist, and determined he must be a "troll" in the group. The criticism and vitriol that stemmed from these women was nothing less than brutish. These are trans women who, historically, have been dismissed and disregarded in feminist circles and have fought for inclusion, yet when a cis male announces he has been advocating for trans rights and issues for over a year, they spew the same dismissal and disregard towards him that has been bestowed upon them. I wonder, then, what these women would have thrown at me if I had chosen to speak up for this man? I am a man, too, one considered as a "traitor" by some cisgender women, having moved into my authentic gender from my birth gender of female. Would I, too, have been attacked with the same viciousness? Instead, I connected with this man and have had several enlightening conversations with him.

The dictionary defines "feminist" as "one who supports feminism", while "ally" is "cooperating / combining / uniting with another for a mutual benefit" (Oxford Dictionary). Where in these definitions does it say that men cannot be feminist, or that cisgender men cannot be trans allies?

It is time to look at the role of transmasculinity in the realm of feminism from the perspective of more than a few transmasculine individuals.

※◇※

Transmasculine Identities and Feminism

In order to understand the intersectionality of feminism and transmasculine identities, one needs to understand the invisible 'borders,' which are profoundly blurred due to innumerable perceptions. Jamison Green, in his book *Becoming a Visible Man*, wrote "I had to understand my part in that system of inequity, whether I occupy a female place and a masculine role or a male place and a masculine role. I needed to understand what it would–really *mean*–to change places: what responsibility would I have for maintaining or deconstructing traditional gender roles once I transitioned? (2004, pg. 23).

One major drawback with understanding feminism has been the misrepresentation by mass media through the last few decades, portraying feminist women as man-haters. It has also perpetuated the myth that all feminists are lesbians. "Simply being lesbian does not make one a feminist, any more than being lesbian makes one political" (hooks, 2000, p. 96). Anderson and Kanner (2009) tackle these myths and emphasize that feminism does not express or promote that idea that men are bad, but instead critiques the underlying systems that produce male domination and privilege, and the stereotypes of male-bashing belittles and trivializes the work involved by these social movements (p. 216).

Eli Green (2006) asserts that like most activist movements, feminism is based on an *identity of oppression*. He states,

> The movement cannot exist without the oppression it seeks to end. While in and of itself this identity is not a negative one, anti-inclusion feminists use an identity of oppression as a shield from trans inclusion and the aforementioned possible undermining of feminist foundations (p. 242).

Transmasculine individuals are commonly rejected for their masculine gender identity – an identity that feminists (as well as lesbians) understand as the transmens' rejection of their own female-sexed bodies and feminine identification. Gayle Rubin reminds us that feminism and lesbian-feminism came about in opposition to a system that imposed rigid roles, and therefore "should not be used to impose new but equally rigid limitations" (2006, p. 479).

Elliot (2004) challenged feminist politics and the question of trans-inclusion, asserting "Transsexuals pose a challenge, intentionally or not, to mainstream feminist conceptions of sex as a stable and immutable basis of gender, a challenge which raises questions about the presumed 'authenticity' of identity and about the inclusiveness of feminist politics" (p. 15). Jamison Green tells us that many trans men who came from the lesbian community were once staunch lesbians with a "highly evolved" feminist consciousness (1998, p. 152).

The number of trans men who consider themselves feminist seems to be high, yet they have been shunned by both cisgender and lesbian feminist circles because they identify as men. A number of these transmasculine individuals have experienced negativity at the mere mention of being a feminist, and the following statements are among several I received in my anonymous questionnaire:

> *I have received hate from trans women and lesbian cis women who told me that men are not allowed to be feminist and transitioning to male is betraying women because men are pigs.* (28, male/man/asexual)

> *Many cis woman have said that I have betrayed women and given into patriarchy by transitioning and therefore can't be a feminist.* (21, male/man, heterosexual/straight)

> *I have been told that I could not be a feminist because I am a man. The person did not know gender identity and did not know that I was not a cis man.* (38, differently-gendered, polysexual)

> *A lot of older women think I should not be a feminist because I abandoned my gender by transitioning to male. I've been told that transgender people in general have no rights in the feminist movement.* (22, transman/FTM, pansexual)

Older trans men, particularly those whose identities were shaped as lesbians during and prior to the second wave of feminism have found themselves on a roller-coaster of social acceptance/non-acceptance, depending on the local community, the year, on new terminologies, and so forth. Many of these individuals were vocal and energetic activists in the fight for women's rights—from the rights to their own body in regards to abortion, domestic abuse, and rape—they fought tirelessly and fearlessly to promote social change.

These individuals were proud to be a part of these changing moments of history, and as mentioned earlier, modeled a highly-evolved feminist consciousness. Because of this feminist consciousness, the term *herstory* came to be an alternative term for relating to the past of these strong, fighting women. Being a feminist, and for many being a lesbian, too, was an integral part of these individual's lives and identities. It was a position of a strong voice, a comradery as strong as any group of individuals could experience, and a position that has historically changed the way society perceived and treated women.

Women-Only Spaces

Of the transmasculine identities I questioned, nearly all agreed that whether or not a trans man could rightfully call himself (or herself) a "lesbian," that considering one's self a lesbian was not an "all-access pass" to lesbian- or women-only spaces. Although some trans men of varying self-identifications do frequent women's bars, support groups and other functions and events, the majority do not. For some, when they began identifying as a man, they removed themselves from the lesbian community either by choice, or because they were rejected because they had crossed that invisible "border" between butch female (or even transbutch), and transman. Others who continued interacting in the lesbian community found an acceptance, and enjoy the diversification of an approving queer community.

I received responses from 142 anonymous transmasculine individuals, who identified across the board with ages, gender and sexual identities, concerning what they thought about trans men in women-only spaces. Three were unsure or had no comment. Fifty-two were against the idea, with answers ranging from "it's inappropriate" and "they can't have it both ways" to "men don't belong in women's space". An overwhelming ninety-three respondents considered the idea and their answers varied from "Whatever floats your boat" and "Not entirely sure, but if it makes them happy" to "It's okay if they are respectful". Many of the ones who were not against it were also clear that they would not enter women's-only spaces personally. I do wish to make it clear that I am not condoning or denying any individual's right to participate in a predominately women-only space with this book, I am simply educating and presenting current phenomenological data.

Before I conclude this section, I feel the need to mention again as I did in Chapter 3, that there are those who consider some butch women part the of trans community, because "Butch women....traverse the boundaries of gender" (Levitt & Heistand, 2004). In these social circles, a butch woman who finds their identification aligns more on the masculine side of the spectrum and embodies the authenticity of man is still a vital part of that circle of friends, regardless of self-identification. The outward presentation and expression may or may not change due to hormones or surgery, but they still represent the same values and beliefs as a person, a human being. If they embody the identification of male, they can be "transbutch" although not all butches take on this identity. Drag king performances, too, which became popular in the 1990s, celebrate genderqueer male sexiness. These transmasculine individuals, regardless of authentic gender identity, (and whether or not they are trans) are generally accepted into women-only spaces. Lesbian culture begins blending with queer/trans culture, and gender boundaries blur even more.

Social Change Must Come From Within

For the longest time, as I mentioned previously, the word "queer" was a derogatory term, but in the 1990s the gay and lesbian community embraced and reclaimed the word; by the early 2000s it was used to denote gender as well as sexuality. At that time, there were many people in the LGBT community who could not or would not agree with the term, and even today there are many who choose not to use it for themselves. The wider majority of individuals who choose to use it as a self-identifying term do not shun, ridicule or get angry at those who choose not to use it. No one seems to have any issues whether someone chooses to use it or not, most people have simply accepted the decisions of others in their use, or non-use of the word.

And now I come once again to the term *herstory*, a predominately "female" word, created by a woman and used by many feminist women. I speak now for a moment to transmasculine identities, specifically those who identify as a man, but also to those who are perceived as men by those around them. First, I encourage you to step in and make a concentrated effort to make changes in wider society. It is men who have formed this patriarchal society, and it is men who need to be responsible for making the necessary changes to help equalize the gendered social order. People have such ingrained, strong cultural ideas of masculinity and femininity that if they perceive someone not conforming, they view that person as "abnormal," "deviant," and not socially legitimate.

With that said, policing those within the trans community, claiming they are not trans because they have *herstory*, or saying they must still be female—only serves to demonstrate that patriarchal dominance is perpetuated even within our own community. We understand there needs to be equality between women and men, and we maintain that men can be feminist alongside of women, but we have to ask ourselves—why does it bother some individuals when someone moves from one category to the other? Are we one of these people who question? If an individual spends twenty years of their life fighting for women's rights, then chooses to take hormones and call themselves "he," does this abolish their entire experience? If they choose to continue to align themselves with the feminist movement, and they are proud of the historical social changes they were a part of effecting, are they now not allowed to talk about their *herstory* like any other individual who embraces the word?

Why must this word *herstory* when used by a transmasculine identity stir up such negativity among both the trans and lesbian communities? Is your outrage due to your own insecurities or your need to control? How does anyone identifying as any gender, sexuality, pronouns, orientations or any other facet of self-identification harm you or your community when you are asking for the same opportunity to claim your own identities? Are we not then, in claiming foul on how someone identifies, perpetuating the oppression we are all claiming to be fighting?

Lastly, I have to ask the same question Leslie Feinberg (1992, p. 148) posited, "Who decided what the 'norm' should be? Why are some people punished for their self-expression?" These individuals have their own individual experiences, and their stories are much like any other stories within the community. I ask you to look within yourselves to seek answers, and remember that social change comes from within. Either it is all for one and one for all, or it is all for nothing.

5

Conversations and Considerations

Some social scientists say that in-group/out-group biases are hard-wired into the human brain. Even without overt prejudice, it is cognitively convenient for people to sort items into categories and respond based on what is usually associated with those categories: a form of statistical discrimination, playing the odds ~ Rosabeth Moss Kanter (2013, para. 3).

As I began my research for this book, I had many conversations with individuals about various aspects I knew were going to predominant in this book. I asked a lot of questions that required deep thought and consideration, and found this was a challenge for some people. Some questions were about thoughts on masculinity and transmasculinity, the gender binary/non-binary, and gender and sexuality. Most spoke of conventional or traditional "expressions," and then upon further prodding, were able to look inside themselves to find answers of what these things meant to them personally.

My questions then became more evocative. Most would react first with their gut or their feelings on a subject, rather than considering the whole concept of the question. For instance, one that generated the most volatile reactions I received, as you can imagine from earlier chapters, came from the scenario of a trans man who identifies as a lesbian. I asked for thoughts on the negativity and discrimination against him from the trans community, and how is that different than what we as a community face from wider society. The immediate reactions were to explain why he would be "wrong" in doing so, and what the "proper" definition of lesbian is, and that "a man can't have his cake and eat it, too" none addressing the actual question. The same type of reactions occurred when I broached the subject of trans men who embraced the word 'herstory', with responses ranging from "Herstory is misgendering of trans men" to "I was never a female, I've always been a male and I have HIStory", to "they aren't really trans, they are butch women." I would then have to point out that the questions were not asking about their thoughts on the *person*, but on *their reaction* to this scenario—how were their feelings dissimilar or more justified than how the general public reacts to any trans person in general.

The deeper contemplations and implications of my questions prompted me to add this chapter to this book due to the respectful conversations evoking various responses, some of which brought up even deeper questions for all to consider. I share these concepts and questions here in order to challenge you to look deeper into your own thoughts, feelings and opinions and try to discern what they might be based upon – fact or fiction, or perhaps the most common, social constructionism.

⬦⬦⬦

My question on the previously-mentioned scenario, asked of people within the wider transmasculine community, stirs up a lot of negativity toward these people who are also within the trans community. These are some of the few, but valid, identities that we have written about in previous chapters, and some of the individuals who have contributed statements or their stories.

Here are the three different scenarios that evoked the most energetic and negative, sometimes radical, reactions. The first is one I wrote more in-depth about in Chapter 3 when I asked about it in a questionnaire;

- Trans men who identify as lesbian
- Trans men who choose to express themselves with feminine clothing or makeup,
- Trans men who embrace the word *herstory* as part of the story of their past lives.

Now this next part is important and I must repeat what I wrote earlier. My questions are not about *them*, it is about *you*—all of us—it is about the wider trans community and the prevailing attitudes regarding these individuals. In other words, I don't want to know *what* you think about these individuals, I want to know *why* you think the way you do, and is there evidence or credible justification for your thoughts.

The following is the wording I used in conversations in addressing the question of reactions to a trans man who chooses to self-identify as lesbian, asking for the implication of discrimination:

> Many within the trans community have been fighting for a long time to break down the gender binary - to remove stereotyping and gender expectations - and have introduced the concepts of a gender spectrum and gender fluidity.
>
> Non-binary and gender-nonconforming individuals do not conform to any set of gender "rules," and many consider themselves trans. They use various pronouns, depending on their comfort level and inner identity on the gender spectrum, yet still remain non-binary and/or non-conforming. Sexual identification has also become less rigid, and terms have been added to cover the vast spectrum of sexual identities, such as pansexual, polysexual and omnisexual, among several others. Terminology has adapted and become comprehensive and inclusive of nearly all genders and sexualities. But have personal ideas and beliefs also adapted? With this in mind, there seems to be a set of "rules" that one must conform to in order to be accepted within the community.
>
> Case in point: The concept of a trans man/guy (gender) who identifies as a lesbian (sexuality) is immediately the target of the gender and sexuality "police." An argument that a "man" cannot be a "lesbian" does not reflect either the belief in removing gender binaries or embracing fluid sexualities, thus rendering both arguments ineffectual.
>
> Does this not indicate binary, inflexible thinking on gender? Does this not negate the idea of multiple sexualities and promote it as theory rather than fact?

You can see my questions are about *perception and bias*. They are about *us*—how *we* feel about those who do not conform to our idea of what is acceptable or not acceptable—and they present the unpleasant idea that in making these judgments, we are perpetuating the very oppression we are trying to eliminate in society. The purpose of the questions are to "prompt" us to look inside ourselves and the things we believe and to question those things. My questions are simply to look at our reasoning for "not feeling comfortable" with people embracing atypical self-identifications, and to question—*why, if we are all on the same "side" of fighting for autonomy and equality, do we continue to perpetuate the problem against our own?* We are creating ingroups and outgroups within our own community, clearly negating the idea of autonomy and equality for which we seek in wider society. In effect, we are limiting ourselves… we accept some of us but not all of us.

Once I was able to direct people past their objections to the idea of whether a trans man can identify as lesbian, which was overall the most difficult part of the conversations, the talk then turned first into discussing the importance, or non-importance, of labels. The trans community as a whole has typically fought against stereotyping labels, and has created new labels for those who did not or would not conform to existing labels. Most people choose labels that suit them, that "feel right" to them. The majority of the discussion participants agreed that it is okay if you don't understand how a label might make sense to someone, and nearly all agreed that telling someone their identity is wrong or invalid is not an option. However, most of those in the discussions had opinions, and there were far more negative views than positive.

One individual had some ideas about labels, since these seem to be what causes the assorted reactions, and he gave permission to share them with you. He wrote,

> *I think ALL labels are our ways to sort things into pieces so we can have predictability. Humans thrive on predictability. It gives us a sense of security. I don't think people are inflexible for labeling. I think they are trying to make order and find security. That's why people are threatened with wrong labels or no labels. It upsets the need for predictability. Those labels can be gender or sexual oriented. They can be value driven like 'pretty' or 'strong' or 'smart.' They can be any adjective we use to try to sort things into the security and comfort of knowing. People who are the most threatened with 'wrong' or 'missing' labels are the people who need the safety and security of predictability more than people who are not threatened.*
> (Connor, 53, ambivalent regarding self-identifying gender labels)

The thought of someone disrupting our sense of comfort is disturbing to us. So we view these people who are making us "feel" uncomfortable as "others," someone not like us, perhaps even unbalanced in their thinking. (As an aside, for the current scenario I saw accusations of 'selfish,' 'immature,' 'privileged' and even the accusation of 'cognitive dissonance.') We fail to realize that whatever labels we adopt for ourselves, and no matter what labels others choose for themselves, we are all just trying to find our place—where we 'fit in.' All of these identity labels, whether gender or sexuality, are merely social constructs—words to which we have given a definition and meaning. That meaning, however, may or may not be exactly the same for all people, and may change at any time.

The absurdity of policing gender was brought up by one person in the discussion, "when gender is understood as an arbitrary construction." Gayle Rubin suggested this idea when she wrote about 'categories' (which is another way of viewing labels), and said of them,

> 'Woman,' 'butch,' 'lesbian,' or 'transsexual' are all imperfect, historical, temporary, and arbitrary. We use them, and they use us. We use them to construct meaningful lives, and they mold us into historically specific forms of personhood. Instead of fighting for immaculate classifications and impenetrable boundaries, let us strive to maintain a community that understands diversity as a gift, sees anomalies as precious, and treats all basic principles with a hefty dose of skepticism (Rubin, 1992, p. 471).

I think that statement sums up what a large portion of us feel about labels, and there is not too much more we can say that isn't covered in the statement. We can all agree that labels, or categories, are socially constructed; and we can all likely agree that we are a diverse community that encompasses a large blanket of labels, and they are unique to each individual. Not everyone agrees on all labels, but the majority respect the assorted terminologies as merely a way to remain inclusive of all genders and sexualities.

Once we made it through the discussion on labels, I again tried to redirect the conversations back to the original questions. I expanded on my original questions in hopes of making them a bit clearer,

Why are these trans men rejected by their own community (the trans community) just because they identify in a non-typical way? These same people are also rejected by the lesbian community, because they are trans, or identify as male. It seems like a difficult place to be if one is simply living authentically. An equally important question would be, why aren't we fighting for their right to identify as they wish? The trans community is fighting for inclusion of other terms and identifications, yet overlooking a segment of individuals within their own community and dismissing them as "not really trans," or worse, "mentally" not quite right in the head - the very things they are fighting against.

Around the same time period I was asking these questions, an example of transgender ingroup/outgroup discrimination appeared in news media. A London trans woman who was given the title of Miss Transgender UK in September of 2015 was recently stripped of her title. Jai Dara Latto identifies as transgender, and plans to have gender reassignment surgery. BBC Three was filming a documentary called "Miss Transgender" where she was seen wearing boxer shorts, and working out at the gym in a t-shirt and shorts. A pageant official decided she was "not trans enough," because she wasn't living full-time as a woman, and declared her a 'drag queen' (Duffy, 2016). Again—because she wore boxer shorts. Need I say anything about how ludicrous this is?

This article did not come up in our discussions, but it was certainly a catalyst for my pressing onwards to continue asking these difficult questions of our community. Interestingly enough, a question arrived from a group member after my initial set of questions that highlights the problem of being told one is 'not trans enough,' and, as well, it applies meanings to labels which assign a set of 'rules' to be included in these labels. If one doesn't conform to these 'rules,' they are seen as 'other' and treated as such.

This newest question was presented as an example of a specific label, 'trans' and the definition that some people attach to the label (i.e. one must experience gender dysphoria to be trans), and if they don't conform to that definition, they aren't "really trans." My reply to this is that I think many people adopt a term for themselves as they enter the community, a term that fits their personal experience, then later, because it IS so personal to them, end up projecting this term as factual for others, whether or not their experience was the same. Because they are so hung up on this now ingrained terminology, they forget that there are other terms and diverse experiences, each of which might be different or the same but they embrace the same term.

I especially saw this as the term transgender became popular, and the huge infighting that occurred due to those who believed themselves to be "true transsexuals." I am seeing the same type of misguided arguments now in the new generations of who is or is not really 'trans'. I think the terms of *trans*, *transgender* and *transsexual* are being conflated by some people in the community, which makes it difficult to discern anyone's actual intent with blanket statements such as "they are less trans than I am," a statement made during this discussion.

✂✂✂

It is well known that trans people face severe discrimination in virtually every aspect of social life. The discrimination is rooted in stereotypes, much the same as those towards women, disabled people, and lesbians, gays, and bisexuals. Stereotyping is one foundation for bias, which in some people takes the form of prejudice and/or discrimination. For a smaller percentage of people, this discrimination exhibits itself in the form of violence or abuse. The statistics of discrimination and its effects on the trans community have been widely published by scores of organizations, websites, social media and individuals over the last several years, so I won't go into it here.

However, I bring this up because this is the 'wider society' discrimination I am comparing to when I bring up these questions regarding the behavior or speech of some individuals in the trans community. Those who exhibit bias against others who don't conform to their beliefs about who is, or isn't, trans, who is "real" and who isn't, who has valid identification labels and who does not. These perceptions and accusations are harmful to the entire trans community, not just to those being discriminated against. They are proof that the oppression we are seeking to eliminate from John Q. Public has wormed its way into our community and it is threatening to perpetuate the same type of hegemonic control or domination we find with men towards women.

It is this ingroup bias I am questioning—the aspect of favoring certain members of the trans community but not others—essentially creating outgroups *within* our community. I read comments and emails on a regular basis from people who are critically depressed, sometimes nearly suicidal, because they've been told they "aren't trans enough" or because they don't experience body dysphoria that they aren't trans at all. I have heard from others who identify as, for instance, trans butch—male-identifying, but don't want surgery and prefer lesbian sexual relationships— but they are not accepted in either the trans community or the lesbian community. They feel they are outcasts, not worthy of an accepting community because they are a 'freak', someone who doesn't socially 'fit' in with either ideology. I have also heard from young, non-binary individuals who consider themselves trans, but have experienced ridicule or rejection from others in the trans community because they express themselves in a traditionally female expression of clothing, hairstyle, painted toenails, et cetera. It is for these people and others that I continue to pursue answers to the really tough questions, in hopes of being a part of effecting needed changes within the community.

※※※

Back to the discussion which prompted this chapter... one individual joined the conversation who was able to provide quite a bit of input. He identifies as an effeminate straight transman, a man who uses male pronouns. However, according to him, his presentation or gender expression doesn't reflect this fact; he prefers clean shaven skin with make-up, long hair, feminine fashion including heels, and long glittery nails.

As he was working towards finding answers for my tough questions, he had this to say as he considered the implications of a trans man who identifies as lesbian, while trying to take into account the importance labels seemingly have for the majority,

> I have no idea how I might feel if I was attached to the title "lesbian" previously, how I might think of changing that with my transition. I think that personally, I would put words as being only worth words and terminology, but I understand that for some people, getting misgendered, having the wrong terminology, or whatever doesn't feel right, can be a massive trigger to their anxiety and Gender Dysphoria issues. But if keeping a certain word is so important to them that it is causing trouble, then wouldn't that be another issue in itself?

> *Being who you are and being free to express your gender is one thing….Lesbian is a very Gender-binary term, as it stands.….Surely, we should not be upset at society for using and keeping a word that shows the gender-binary evolution of civilization? I guess I do not feel correct in taking such a well-defined word that is binary and particular in definition, and using it because it appeases a form of anxiety or self-doubt in myself, unless I was truly Gender Neutral, and the word could in at least some context apply. I do believe in freedom, but I do not believe in taking everything and molding it to one's image to achieve that freedom. I believe in creation and invention, addition to the culture, enrichment of it, rather than complete change.* (Arseni, 21, FTM)

We continued this line of thought by considering that since 'lesbian' is a socially-constructed gender-specific term, what is the difference with men such as him who present themselves in traditionally feminine attire, this also being a social construct. In other words, how is the aspect of a trans man presenting as female perceived differently than one whose core identity is lesbian?

Arseni's answer was again subjective and well thought out.

> *How is it different to me? Well, that is entirely dependent on how the femininity is expressed. I express with outwards decorations, such as aesthetics, not with biology, and not with pronouns or classifications. A transman that has their core identity as lesbian could be like me, could be a hard masculine, it could be anyone, and that is why it's so hard to define for me. I could be that person, all it takes is for me to decide lesbian is the right term for me. So could a lumberjack-looking fella with a thick beard. In the gender neutral, or gender queer community, gender and terminology becomes as fluid as water, and changes with every day, but that is how you define these people.*
>
> *If a bearded, lumberjack person came up to me and presented themselves with feminine pronouns and identified as a lesbian, I would not be opposed to accepting such. That is the very same as me walking up to someone with my dark maroon lipstick and saying "Hello, I am Mister [name removed], pleasure to meet you." In a personal situation, I would not object.*
>
> *Where my thoughts would begin to wonder is, why, if we are so*

adamant on being free with our gender expression, are the binary terms even still valued? That becomes the next debate. Once we were to all fully accept that any term can be applied to anyone, it becomes how we are going to further define these terms so that they have application.

The entire need to gender identify and label sexualities is perhaps attached to the need to understand and make the unknown, known. What we need to strive for in a society, is having the idea that gender and sexuality are infinite and not stuck in stone…When gender fluidity is innate and no longer something that requires questioning and wondering, we won't need to worry about hate, let alone labels….With true Gender neutrality, I wouldn't feel there is as much of an issue, because I understand the fluidity of gender neutral people and how they can swing from feminine and masculine freely…. Perhaps the issue is in exactly how gender binary the trans community actually really is. (Arseni, 21, FTM)

Is it possible that he has just touched on the problem *and* the solution? It is the concept of a truly *gender neutral* society—that for which the trans community has been so strongly advocating where gender isn't the driving factor for nearly every facet of daily life. Yet, many are unwilling to adapt to changes or terminologies because it might upset others, or it doesn't "feel good." Meanings are interpreted and perceived due to social acceptance or non-acceptance. Stereotypes and bias end up making the rules. Which brings us back to the questions of the discrimination within our own community.

Why do some trans people feel they have the right to tell others they aren't "trans enough," or how they should or should not self-identify? We are constantly having our validity as trans people called into question by society, yet we do the same within the community to others. Why are we creating power dynamics where some trans people are inherently 'better', 'more worthy', 'more trans', or in some way 'more important' or 'more deserving' than other trans people. That, to me, is creating social hierarchies within our community, exerting privilege and power over others. We are taking away their right to self-identify, and this is not indicative of social justice. In creating levels of transness, we are giving the rest of society permission to misgender us. Why should they believe us, when we can't even believe in each other? We have become "gender police," and we have brought the very thing we've been fighting against—oppression—into our community.

There must be an effective solution. And this solution *must* be inclusive of all individuals who identify as trans, transgender, transsexual, non-binary, and all other forms of gender nonconformity. It is imperative that we stop tearing each other apart, which serves only to create power dynamics that seem to indicate some trans people are 'better' or 'more real'—this is not social justice.

If the trans community truly wants autonomy and equality, then I suggest fighting for this total inclusion, and cease putting stipulations on who is, or isn't, 'worthy.' First work inside of our community, then let the voices of the strong majority take the fight into wider society. Arseni puts it like this, "We should by all means be fighting to respect and defend everyone under the non-binary umbrella, because they suffer the same stipulation as the binary-trans community—They are going against conventional gender roles, and being discriminated against because of it."

There are no right or wrong answers, but there are solutions. It is up to us as a community to find them. Another transman puts it into perspective for us when he states,

> People have been successfully changing the ideas of a majority since the beginning of time. It takes a movement to effect change, however. As an example, Galileo was not able to affect change by himself. He was forced to recant and lived under house arrest the remainder of his life. It took a movement by the scientific community to convince the majority. It will take a community of us to effect change too, and our sisters will keep dying at alarming rates at the hands of fear until we do....A minority is the majority of an even smaller minority. As detestable as it is, until a minority feels empowered, it will divide and conquer. That being said, our sense of self and community are evolving in positive ways, as is society's view of us. Let us give ourselves some pats on the back for these positive strides. This is true empowerment. (Theron, 59, Transman)

There is nothing more I can add to this powerful statement. I can only ask our community, as well as the rest of society, to open hearts and minds to the diversity within, and recognize that we are all valid human beings.

6

The Conflicts and Choices
in Being Men

Nothing upsets the underpinnings of feminist fundamentalism more than the existence of transsexuals. A being with male chromosomes, a female appearance, a feminist consciousness, and a lesbian identity explodes all of their assumptions about the villainy of men. And someone with female chromosomes who lives as a man strikes at the heart of the notion that all women are sisters, potential feminists, natural allies against the aforementioned villainy. (Patrick Califia, in E. Green, 2006, p. 232).

Hegemony. Patriarchy. Misogyny. Oppression. Male privilege.

These are the things that are ever prevalent in society, and they stem from men. Young men, older men, cisgender men—and yes, even trans men. What are these words that evoke such strong emotion in all genders? What do they mean, and how did we, as transmasculine individuals, end up being lumped into a category wrought with such unpleasant terminology? Since we have plunged into this vast domain called 'masculinity' and it is where we feel we belong, what can we do to acknowledge, address and argue against the constant reinforcement of the attitudes, behaviors and actions we witness inside this socially constructed category called 'men'?

If men are indeed the problem, and with many transmasculine individuals presenting, expressing and/or identifying themselves as men, how (or perhaps, why) do we then fit into the 'bigger picture' when we are being accused of the very things we have experienced first-hand during our former lives as perceived females? Whether or not we considered ourselves a feminist, whether or not we ever felt like a girl or a woman; the plain, hard truth is that we were born into, and socialized into, the role of 'female.' We, as transmasculine individuals, have all experienced the oppression and misogyny; if not on an individual level, then certainly on a group level—the 'group' (or category) being a member of the 'female' half of society.

In identifying and presenting on the masculine side of the gender spectrum, which is generally and often considered socially as more 'masculine' than feminine, we are unintentionally thrust into a position that doesn't always feel comfortable for us. Even for those of us who appear more feminine yet are perceived as male in society, we find ourselves questioning what masculinity means *to* us and *for* us, and find confusion, and a variety of other answers as you read in Chapter 3. We find ourselves in a position that, even we feel this is where we need to be, is distressing when we realize the implications. Shaddon (2016) explains these implications in the social context as, "Masculinity, then, is privileged over femininity in that sense, for if men and women are opposites, then so must masculinity and femininity; and if they are opposites, one must represent strength, power, authenticity, and the other must be weakness, fragility, and artificial" (p. 114).

Hegemonic Masculinity

Suddenly, in being perceived as men, we have entered into a situation that seems to contradict everything we abhorred and detested about being perceived as female, because now *we* are the ones who are considered the perpetrators. We have become a part of *hegemonic masculinity* (Connell, 2005), a concept denoting the dominant social position of men over the subordinate social position women in society. "*Hegemonic masculinity* is defined by the image of those men in power, such that masculinity requires being power, aggressive, competitive, strong, successful, capable and in control" (Glotfelter, 2012, pp. 28-29).

"But, wait!" you say, "I'm not a man in power. I'm not aggressive!" It does not matter, because society's rigid perception of that *image* trumps your more realistic perception of yourself. Face it, society as we know it is a rigid and age-old structure of male-domination. Once we step out visibly into the *roles* and *appearances* of masculinity, regardless if we are gentlemen or abusers, we have assumed a position in the grander scheme of it all and we are 'branded.' The ideologies of masculinity or manhood may not be an accurate representation of all men, yet they are perceived as such, and are widespread and all-encompassing by many people, particularly those of half the members of society—the women.

The concept of *hegemony* is really a very simple one. Merriam-Webster (2016) defines it as "the social, cultural, ideological, or economic influence exerted by a dominant group." Hegemony in our culture is what allows for oppression and misogyny, and is what condones and perpetuates male privilege. Hegemony can be imposed upon marginalized groups and is what patriarchy lives for—men asserting power and control over women. It is also consensual—it is a process of consent, resistance, and coercion. Hegemony works because people at every level of the hierarchical society accept it without question or challenge. Williams (1977) defines it as, "It is a whole body of practices and expectations, over the whole of living: our senses and assignments of energy, our shaping perceptions of ourselves and our world" (p. 110).

"Ok," you say next, "what about patriarchy? It means that men rule society, right? Where do I fit into this? I was born and socialized as a female, so I understand that and oppose it, and I'm not any different now than I was then! Why am I being penalized by women and praised by men just because my identity or outward presentation has changed?"

Yes, patriarchy by its very definition is a *males-are-in-power* concept, and because of the hegemonic structure of society, we are provided with a male-dominated, patriarchal culture. When we were perceived as women, we were the 'lesser than' and the 'subordinate'—we were the oppressed. No matter how hard we strove to get ahead, we were constantly facing the barriers constructed by men in our struggles to get ahead. The lower wages, the 'glass ceilings,' the victims of harassment, sexism and abuse, the expectations of becoming a housewife or a teacher or an office assistant rather than the CEO of a major corporation or a construction worker or famous athlete—these were the hurdles and obstructions we were forced to work around in order to achieve our goals. Sadly, many of us, *as is the case for the majority of women worldwide*, were unable to even get close to our goals because of the oppression that faced us on a near-daily basis. Those who found their way through or around it faced a whole other aspect of oppression; those comments, actions and behaviors reserved by some men to dismiss and rebuke women who do manage to succeed.

Before I leave these concepts of hegemony and patriarchy and dive into the other terminologies, I want to leave you with a couple of thoughts. Previously, I wrote that hegemony is consensual, and I will follow that statement with—patriarchy is *also* consensual. "Patriarchy cannot exist without the adherence to its tenets by both females, who are the subjugated, and males, who subjugate" (Kallahan, 2014, para. 16). I want to clarify, however, with my statements I am not claiming that all women are accepting of the position men have attempted to place then into, nor am I claiming that all men are the culprit and deserve to be considered the enemy. There are some women who spend their lives fighting the stereotypes and oppression from men (many being feminists), and there are a lesser number of men who challenge the patriarchal system by allying themselves with these women in the fight for the recognition that all people are human beings and deserve equal respect.

Lerner (1986) writes about patriarchy and the role women have in this system, and states,

> The system of patriarchy can function only with the co-operation of women. This cooperation is secured by a variety of means: gender indoctrination; educational deprivation; the denial to women of knowledge of their history; the dividing of women, one form the other, by defining "respectability" and "deviance" according to women's sexual activities; by restraints and outright; coercion; by discrimination in access to economic resources and political power; and by awarding class privileges to conforming women (p. 217).

I bring this up because we, as transmasculine individuals, need to have a basic understanding of not only where we came from but also where we fit into society now. In knowing this, we can continue to learn more about the aspects—the positives and the negatives—of being male in society.

Misogyny / Transmisogyny

The dictionary defines *misogyny* as "hatred, dislike, or mistrust of women, or prejudice against women" (Dictionary.com, 2016). It can be manifested in many ways, including, but not limited to, sexual discrimination, belittling of women, hostility, violence and sexual objectification. Misogyny is always sexist in nature, and is commonly heard in men's gathering places, such as locker rooms and sporting events, but it also shows up in board rooms and political platforms. It permeates throughout society, sometimes insidious and at other times blatant and deliberate. Misogyny affects everyone of all genders. Julia Serano (2007) talks about it in her various writings, describing misogyny as "the tendency to dismiss and deride femaleness and femininity." This not only devalues women, but also *any* expression of femininity—including that from trans men and gender non-conforming individuals. "Misogyny is a cage for everyone—as long as women aren't free, men won't be, either" (Berlatsky, 2014, para. 9).

Transmisogyny is a relatively new term, first written about in detail by Julia Serano in her book *Whipping Girl* in 2007. At that time, the term meant a discrimination or prejudice against transgender women, but since that time the definition has expanded to cover all gender nonconforming individuals. In order to fully comprehend 'transmisogyny,' however, one must understand not only 'misogyny' as defined previously, but also the meaning of the term 'transphobia.'

Transphobia is defined as emotional disgust, irrational fear, hatred, or discrimination towards individuals who do not conform to binary gender norms (Glotfelter, 2012, p. 6). It is the discrimination of, and negative attitudes towards trans people based on their gender expression. The term corresponds to the word 'homophobia,' and indicates that fear is the main component of someone's reaction involving prejudice, discrimination and/or violence towards trans people (Winter, 2010). Transphobia reflects a hatred of any who do not fit into or conform to either side of the gender binary.

Put transphobia and misogyny together, and you come up with the term *transmisogyny*, and this is the foundation for severe discrimination, abuse, violence, and extreme hatred of any individual of any gender, gender expression or gender identity who does not embody the binary of masculine and feminine. Transmisogyny exhibits itself not only in the wider population towards trans people (as well as towards lesbian, gay and bisexuals who exhibit perceived deviations from binary), but it also is reflected within the LGBT community, including deeper within the trans community itself. Some lesbians and gay men struggle with their issues with trans people, and some trans people are unaccepting of others in their own community who present or exhibit their gender differently than they do. "Trans and gender non-conforming people who do not necessarily identify as women, but who present feminine characteristics and/or identify along the feminine end of the gender spectrum are also on the receiving end of transmisogyny" (Kacere, 2014, para. 7). This includes it being directed at men—both cisgender men and trans-identi-fied men who present more to the feminine side than the masculine. This also includes those who choose not to take hormones or surgically alter their bodies, yet still identify as a man—because society will undoubtedly make assumptions and misgender them, placing them in the constructs of 'female.' This occurs even after being corrected, because at that mo-ment when the misgendering continues, it becomes a form of trans-misogyny.

I bring up transmisogyny now as I reflect on misogyny, because I would like to think that in showing how these both apply to transmas-culine individuals, it may engender a greater understanding of the need for trans men to *actively engage* in the pursuit of radically modifying, or perhaps even eliminating, the social constructs of gender that currently serve as the vehicles for discrimination and hate.

What are some examples of misogyny and transmisogyny we see in our daily lives? I mentioned one instance, in the form of intentionally misgendering someone after being informed of their authentic gender. This is a common occurrence both inside and outside of the trans com-munity; not only do those in the general public refuse to acknowledge one's identity and pronouns, but also there are those within the commu-nity itself who are guilty of this, those who consider themselves "more trans" because they have taken hormones or had surgeries.

Other examples include commonly heard words and phrases, such as 'Nice tits,' 'Hey, Baby,' and 'You're hot,' as well as 'You throw like a girl,' 'What a bitch,' 'Be a man—not a sissy,' and 'She's a ball-buster.' In trans circles, common phrases include 'You're not really trans if you don't have lower surgery,' 'Trans women are too aggressive,' and 'You don't know what living as a male is really like, you still look like a female.' More severe phrases include 'She was asking for it wearing that short skirt,' 'If she hadn't drank so much alcohol, she wouldn't have put herself into that position in the first place,' and 'Slut!' while transmisogynists might be inclined to say 'You're not trans enough' (a commonly heard phrase in the trans community), 'What did you expect when you still look like a female?' or 'Get over yourself and grow a pair!'. There is another phrase that some trans men are attempting to reclaim and use in a positive man-ner, 'Man up,' but this term is still widely considered a form of oppres-sion, and I believe it is one that needs eliminated from our vocabulary along with the other harmful words and phrases. One last example might be a transmasculine space that allows butch cisgender women, but turns away trans butch women, or a transfeminine support group that turns away a more masculine-appearing, yet gender non-conforming individual.

All of these phrases and many more are not only sexist, they are a form of misogyny or transmisogny—a gendered act of separating men and women, the masculine and feminine—while enforcing that the female aspect is "lesser than" that of the male, or that one way or experience of being trans is better than another way or experience. In our sexist society, being a woman or gender non-conforming automatically places you in a position of 'less value,' and this is particularly true when observing some transmasculine-identified individuals who have come from a place of hate towards any representation of 'female.'

I wanted to know what contemporary transmasculine individuals thought about misogyny, having considered that many were not around during the Second wave of feminism, and some were only just born when the Third wave came around, so I asked in an informal survey. The questions were phrased as,

> What are your personal thoughts on misogyny? Have you taken measures around those displaying this tendency to help stop their behaviors and actions that prevent the oppression and/or contempt for women and transgender individuals? **Have you ever been accused of being misogynistic?**

In adding the last question, I did not really expect anyone to admit to having been called out on misogynistic behavior, but I wanted to be inclusive. I left these questions open-ended in order to get as true and thorough answers as possible, and was surprised at the honesty from some of the participants. I am now even more convinced that additional education is needed for those within our own community.

Out of 89 transmasculine individuals 14-65 years old who responded to these three questions on misogyny,

- 4 were not sure what misogyny is (with one of them claiming the behavior isn't "as much misogyny as it is individual people being dicks")
- 7 had no experience whatsoever with misogyny, (with one who called it "childish")

- 11 stated either they had not experienced it, or misogyny was "disgusting", "screwed up", "stupid" or "annoying"
- 12 admitted having issues with their own misogynistic thoughts or behaviors
- 20 indicated to having witnessed misogyny around them or were the target of someone's statements
- 35 indicated having witnessed it and had called someone out on it or educated those around them at least once

I have challenged both trans and cisgender men who make misogynistic statements and received both genuine contemplations of what I have said, as well as defensive and verbally abusive reactions. For those who listened, I can only hope they took the small grain of truth I implanted in them and cultivated it so it could grow. For those who were defensive, I can only say that I will not stop; if I hear it again, I will repeat my objections. I truly believe that the only way we as transmasculine individuals can make even a small dent in our patriarchal system is to challenge other men—both cis and trans—in our daily lives, and not remain silent when we witness these words, actions and behaviors.

Male Privilege

When I am discussing patriarchy, misogyny, or sexism, I am referring to a system of *oppression.* A system that automatically, because of its very nature of placing men in a higher social status than women, oppresses the female half of the human species as well as those who do not conform to binary standards. Johnson (2005) says of oppression, "whenever one social category is privileged, at least one other category is oppressed" and describes oppression as,

> A social phenomenon that happens between different groups in a society. It is a system of social inequality through which one group is positioned to dominate and benefit from the exploitation and subordination of another (p. 136).

Male privilege is something that extends to all men, but in different ways, and "privilege exists when one group has something of value that is denied to others simply because of the groups they belong to, rather than because of anything they've done or failed to do" (Johnson, 2005, p. 23). Privilege and oppression both are seen at the group or category level, rather than at the individual level. When a man is accused of benefitting from male privilege, it is the privilege that is automatically granted to a category, in this case, males. As transmasculine individuals begin to be seen as males on a social level, they have automatically been granted this "privilege," but it is not necessarily the kind of 'privilege' they desire.

The dictionary defines the word privilege as "a right, immunity, or benefit enjoyed only by a person beyond the advantages of most" (Dictionary.com, 2016), and 'male privilege' is a concept that examines social, economic, and political advantages or rights which are made available to men simply because they *are* men. Zitz, Burns and Tacconelli state , "A paradox is alluded to where physically 'passing' as male, the desired identity, automatically brings with it the undesired identification with hegemonic male privilege. Male privilege is discoursed as being intersected by other dimensions such as race and sexuality, with the heterosexual, white male being the most privileged" (2014, p. 25).

Male privilege is a direct result of patriarchy.

I emphasize this in order to help frame the concept when we as transmasculine individuals are accused of having male privilege, and how, if we are perceived socially as men, we are automatically granted this rite of passage into manhood whether we wanted it or not, or even if we do not understand it completely. In my research for this book, I have found that the concept of male privilege is something that is mostly understood by a percentage of transmasculine individuals, and is also something that many of them agree it is unfortunate that this occurs in society.

I questioned 94 transmasculine individuals in a survey on their experiences with male privilege. These participants ranged from 15 to 65 years old. The questions were open-ended, and they were able to answer as much or as little as they felt comfortable in sharing. The questions were phrased as:

> Do you have any specific thoughts on how you have experienced, or not experienced, male privilege? Have you encountered any negatives? Positives? What are your

thoughts on this phenomena in general throughout society?

Considering most trans men do not experience male privilege until they are seen or perceived as men in society, it was not surprising to find that approximately 35% fell into this category. However, 15.95% of them seem to be in need of education on this facet of the patriarchal system. Here are the results of this line of questioning:

- 3 had nothing at all to say about it
- 15 seemed to be either confused about what male privilege actually is, or denying that it exists, or agreeing it exists but unable to explain
- 33 had not experienced it, with "not passing yet" as the most common reason
- 43 have experienced male privilege, most often stating the benefits, but also with a few of the negative aspects included.

More often than not, those who have experienced male privilege expressed the positives as: Being taken more seriously, wage increases, a cessation of harassment (such as "cat calls" from cisgender men), and they are treated with more respect. The negatives included; they are now being seen as a strange man around children, women are more fearful of them, and the experience of the 'loss' of the safe space with women, among other situations that were seen as a negative consequence.

One younger participant answered with the following:

> I never expected the privilege I have gotten. I get twice as much food in the University cafeteria than girls without asking. I don't feel afraid walking down the street alone or at night. This girl asked me to walk her to the dorms on art night. I was really confused because I thought of myself as at the same risk as her, but my beard means I can, and should, protect her. Girls are scared of me. They won't hang out alone with me and they walk on the opposite side of the street. One time, I was in the laundromat reading while my clothes dried. This girl walked in and was startled and went to get her friend, who told me I can't hang out in there because I'm creepy. I am a threat and that is heart breaking. (Anonymous, 23,

Transman)

While another older individual stated:

> *I had no idea. I thought I did. But, wow, male privilege is unbe-*
> *lievable. Obviously, it works out just dandy for me most of the time*
> *as a white person read as male all the time. Customer service has*
> *never been better. Also, without any additional education or skill-*
> *sharing, I apparently am now an expert on all things navigation*
> *and anything to do with [my workplace]. I am assuming that this*
> *is knowledge that all dudes are just expected to possess somehow.*
> (Anonymous, 44, Transman)

Although many of the individuals who admitted to experiencing male privilege made a point of stating they were not entirely
comfortable with the concept, they concurred they were benefitting from it. Additionally, there are the ones who, like the following, not only recognize their privilege, but enjoy it immensely,
although they agree it is something which needs "amended" in
society. The following individual seems to believe that women
somehow have 'privilege,' which is a belief I have seen mentioned or suggested by more than person;

> *I am a white male and have noticed a significant difference in the*
> *way the world view me as a male now. I realized I have finally*
> *found my place in the world and love it. I don't approve of white*
> *male privilege, of course, but I am accepting of the fact that it exists*
> *and is something society needs to amend. I have also noticed a level*
> *of privilege that women have and that has been eye opening.*
> (Anonymous, Male/man, 53)

Lastly, I want to mention one particular reaction to the mere *mention*
of male privilege by a very young man. It is obvious to me he is not only
confused, but also very angry. He wrote,

> *I don't really understand what the whole "male privilege" thing is*
> *about. I mean, I know obviously there's still sexism in our back-*
> *wards society, but just because it's a little harder to be a woman*
> *doesn't mean that it's a breeze being a dude. What I hate is how*
> *the so-called 'feminists' that hate trans men for no reason say that*

trans guys are "women just trying to get male privilege." What? So I'd go through this whole transition just to get a little more income, etc.? These idiots have to realize that it's WAY harder to be a trans guy than to be a woman. I don't really care about this whole "male privilege" thing for myself—all I want to do is "pass" as male and being called "sir" and "he" out in public. That's not "male privilege," that's just being seen as who I am—a guy. (Anonymous, Male/man, 16)

There was also an older man who, after decades of living as female before transition, now felt that male privilege was not as apparent or widespread now as it was when he was younger. I am not certain that this person, like many others, truly understands the depth or expanse of male privilege. It is quite apparent by these kinds of answers, and others which were similar in their dismissal or rejection of the idea of male privilege, that education is needed among the transmasculine community.

Examples of Male Privilege

With nearly 16% of respondents who were not completely understanding what male privilege is, or even admitting they have no idea whatsoever, I think it is important to share some random, generic examples to highlight this phenomenon. I believe there are a multitude of experiences that aren't always seen as a product of male privilege, and perhaps shedding some light on them might be of some benefit to those who question.

- You are less likely to be a victim of stalking
- You are less likely to be the victim of domestic abuse
- You are less likely to be a victim of rape or other sexual assault
- You can walk at night without a buddy with you
- You will likely not be 'blamed' for being a victim because of what you were wearing
- You can go topless and show your nipples in public
- Your behaviors, such as swearing and interrupting are likely to go unchallenged
- You are taken more seriously, even if you are saying

the same thing that a woman says

- You can be non-monogamous without damaging your 'reputation' or be called a 'slut'
- Your statements are less likely to be challenged, since you are seen as more credible
- You aren't interrupted
- You will likely make more money doing the exact same job as a woman
- You don't experience "cat calls" and inappropriate whistling and statements about your body when you walk by
- You are more likely to be served faster and treated with respect in restaurants
- You are more likely sought out by store employees offering to help you find something
- You are more likely to pay less than a woman would for the same automobile at a dealership

For the purpose of brevity, I will refrain from going on for what could be several dozen more examples of the privilege bestowed upon men in society. An Internet search on the phrase "examples of male privilege" should keep you busy learning for part of an afternoon.

The Dual Perspectives of Transmasculine Individuals

Many trans men are in the unique position of having been socially gendered as both women and men. Not all trans men choose to honor their past, and will oppose any suggestion of their previous female experience. For many, leaving the female/feminine past behind cannot happen fast enough. Many harbor extreme anger at having been forced to be a girl, then socialized as a woman. Some believe they were never really female, they were always male and the world just couldn't see it. Others believe they were socialized as female, but, being male-identified, they challenged and bucked the system. Still others lived their lives as girls, then women, and went into a heterosexual marriage, while many found themselves embracing the lesbian community.

Before I delve too far into the dual perspectives of trans men in our male-dominated society, I feel it is necessary to continue to explore the diversity of attitudes towards life prior to being socially recognized as male, as I would argue that *some* of these attitudes are, at least partially, the culprit of confusion, lack of awareness, and even certain behaviors in regards to male privilege and misogyny/transmisogyny in the community. Some of those who have dismissed their experiences prior to their lives now as men reject any inference to femininity, so much so they become *hypermasculine*, embracing not only the positives of being male, but also contributing to negative stereotypes.

Hypermasculinity is an extreme example of behaviors, thoughts, words and actions thought to be 'male.' It excludes fluid and ambiguous ways of being a man, and reflects a fear of loss of male social power. It manifests itself in various ways including aggressiveness, loudness, misogynistic, macho-ness, engaging in crude sexual talk about women, controlling, and even violent. In other words, hypermasculinity is a form of *overcompensation* for all men, and is a perfect example of what *not* to be. It is common for trans men to display hypermasculinity early in their transition (Abelson, 2014, p. 45), but most tend to *soften* into just a 'regular guy' once they begin 'passing' full-time (being perceived as) as men in society.

Dozier (2005) published a study on a small group of trans men in order to facilitate understanding of their experiences by investigating the changing behaviors and interactions during transition. It was noted that as they had become "socially recognized as men, they tended to be more comfortable expressing a variety of behaviors and engaging in stereotypically feminine activities, such as sewing or wearing nail polish. The increase in male sex characteristics creates both greater internal comfort with identity and social interactions that are increasingly congruent with sex identity. As a result, some FTMs are able to relax their hypermasculine behavior" (p. 305).

There are numerous transmasculine individuals who choose to embrace both their masculine and feminine sides. One young individual gave his thoughts on the dichotomy of his two separate life experiences, explaining how they intersect for him,

> *Well, I believe being a transmasculine male has its benefits for me at least, because I've lived for 22 years in a woman's body, and I have experienced being a woman majority of my life and then realizing my truth; and starting living my life as a man, I have the best of both worlds. Even though I wasn't a feminine woman I was a strong, Black, independent woman, and I was proud of that and*

now, living as a black man, I'm even prouder because I understand that I don't need to fit in this stereotypical 'box' of what black men should act like. I don't need to be over-aggressive to get my point across, or put on this macho facade. I can be authentic. Isn't that what this journey is about—being who you're supposed to be regardless of the odds? So for me, my masculinity and femininity are the same—they co-exist—giving me a balance within myself that I'm proud of. I'm a gentle soul who takes no shit, LOL. (Sean, 22, Transman)

Although this facet of embracing both the masculine and feminine in the transmasculine experience has not yet been thoroughly studied, from personal observations I can attest to the fact that it is not uncommon; however, it has not been *shown* or *verbalized* in demonstrably high numbers. I do not know if this is due more to the fact that a greater percentage of individuals deny their relationship to their former lives, or if some have chosen to remain quiet about this area of their lives in fear of being ridiculed or rejected by their peers. I tend to think it is the latter, mainly due to the answers to more probing questions I continue to ask, and from the occasional private message or email I would receive from those who did, indeed, embrace their feminine side, but chose not to disclose this to peers. Again, this would highlight the transmisogyny which permeates throughout the trans community.

Marval A Rex, a 24-year-old transmasculine individual had top surgery in early 2016 and wrote publicly about his experiences during the first seven days after surgery. In considering the masculine and the feminine, on the second day he wrote,

I felt sweet and soft and sugary after top surgery. I felt feminine in this bizarrely ironic way.....I do not fear the feminine, as many assume of those who seek top surgery. I have cleared the way for my feminine, taken great and sometimes calculated risks to reach her, and believe in her energy as she heals my broken-to-wholeness body. I do not fear her. I know, resolutely, that the feminine is the future. That which is Feminine appears inside all bodies of all expressions, and does not demand any constricting labels to satisfy her. She is within all of us, regardless of our self-definitions and personal stories. Her gentle power sits inside all of us, often dormant but with patience unsurpassable. She can work through all of us; be gentle and kind and open us up to ourselves. This feminine nature will

> *heal a sickly world of fear-based limitations, spawned from of a false sense of control. The collective schizophrenia brought about by a masculine imbalance of "do, do, do" "make, make, make" "conquer, conquer, conquer" will dissolve under the warmth of her embrace. I reclaim the feminine. I reclaim love over fear. I reclaim my body.* (Marval, 24, Transmasculine/Genderqueer)

Whether one chooses to accept or reject their past lives, the fact remains that transmasculine individuals first experienced their lives as girls, then as women with female embodiments. They have each been exposed to the oppressions which women and girls are subjected, to varying extents and depending on their racial, ethnic, class, geographical positions (Hale, 1998). These experiences, wanted or not wanted, recognized or not recognized, clearly separates trans men from cisgender men in their ability to understand the oppression of women. They, too, "*remain* marginalized and thus oppressed in a society that engenders them unintelligible" (Noble, 2006, emphasis added).

In his book, *Masculinities*, Connell (1995) speaks of the "patriarchal dividend"—the advantages men in general gain from the subordination of women—and although not born into this phenomena, trans men are not immune to it. Once an individual 'crosses over' into being socially recognized as a man, he is automatically awarded a respect, authority and prestige he has not previously experienced. More significant, however, is the recognition that this *also* gives trans men an advantage over those assigned male at birth—that of the cognizance and awareness that this has occurred, and they have a choice in how they will respond to it.

We must learn from the past if we are to be able to participate with the present.

Knowing that men are the gatekeepers for gender equality, we as transmasculine individuals are equally responsible for reform—reconstruction and transformation. It is imperative that we grasp our sense of agency and realize the importance of initiating, executing and controlling our own volitional actions in the world in order to effect what could only be positive change. "True solidarity with the oppressed means fighting at their side to transform the objective reality which has made them...'beings for another'...To affirm that men and women are persons and as persons should be free, and yet to do nothing tangible to make this affirmation a reality, is a farce" (Gately, 2010, p. 4, citing Freire, 1993, pp.

49-50)

I believe we as transmasculine individuals have the *responsibility* to strive towards the elimination of all oppressive language and behaviors that patronize, objectify, and penalize not only women, but all who do not conform to the gender binary. We have *all* experienced this patriarchal domination, whether or not we accepted it or were subservient to it. Whether we were blind to it, or ignored it, or if we fought it and struggled for our right to be human beings, equal and able—patriarchy existed (and still does) as the dominant force in our lives.

We have the opportunity to be the catalyst for future change. We can *choose* to remember, and we can *choose* to take responsibility. We can *take action* in our daily lives, by calling out other men when we witness any language or act of oppression. We can *choose* to avoid hypermasculinity, and we can *choose* to distance ourselves from the hegemonic domination, by symbolically and in practice, giving up our 'power.'

I will end this chapter with a short paragraph from the authors of *Scripting Masculinity*, who assert that *fluidity of gender* could dissolve gender entirely, which, in essence, would be creating a world without systems of gender oppression.

> If we take the fluidity of gender identities to its logical conclusion, it would simply dissolve. Thus the fluidity of gender identities could be expressed not in terms of adopting positions in between masculinity and femininity, but in terms of dissolving into 'not gender'. Fluidity here would refer to gender moving beyond its frame, disappearing, no longer being contained by additional types of femininities or masculinities; it would open up the possibility for the dissolution of gender categories. Therefore if we retain the notion of fluidity, it would be to express the partial hold that gender exercises on identities and social relations, as well as its partial relevance in understanding social relations (Fournier & Smith, 2006, p. 158).

I maintain my belief that we can transform the world as we know it by purposefully and willingly confront misogyny, transmisogyny, and oppressions by any other name, because "masculinities come into existence as people act. They are accomplished in everyday conduct or organizational life, as configurations of social practice" (Connell, 1996, p. 210).

It is up to us to *choose to act* like responsible and conscious human beings with an aversion to inequity.

7

Mourning the Losses
—Facing the Fears

*For me, it was never a question of whether or not I was transgender.
It was a question of what I'd be able to handle transitioning and
having to do it in the public eye. One of the issues that was hard
for me to overcome was the fear of that.* ~ Chaz Bono (Sachs,
2011, para. 8).

*I have learned over the years that when one's mind is made up, this
diminishes fear; knowing what must be done does away with fear.*
~ Rosa Parks

I do not believe this book could be complete without including the universal theme of loss as well as the fears that many trans people experience. You'll find it in some of the upcoming stories from the Contributors that loss is a common experience in the process of becoming ourselves. Coming out as trans or gender non-conforming is one of the single most difficult things a person has to do in their life, for in doing so they risk rejection by the people they love. 57% of trans people have experienced some level of family rejection, and 58% had lost at least one friendship. Other losses include the loss of employment as well as housing, with one in five trans people being denied housing, 11% others being evicted and another 19% experiencing homelessness at some point in their lives because they chose to live authentically (Grant, Mottet & Tanis, 2009).

Many will agonize over the moment of embarking on the journey to authenticity for weeks, months or even years in advance of actually doing it. Many wonder if they will lose their family, friends, their partner, their home—will they be hated, rejected, despised? Many, too, entertain suicidal thoughts, wondering if it might be the easier alternative. Forty-one percent of trans people attempt suicide compared to just over one and a half percent of the general population, and higher percentages of attempts for those who lost jobs and income, or were harassed or assaulted—up to sixty-four percent (Grant, et al.).

In the years I have been in the trans community, many of them working through my non-profit organization, *TransMentors International*, I have witnessed countless individuals agonizing over the 'coming out trans' process. They are understandably anxious about every facet of their lives and how they will be affected. Some worry about personality changes when taking Testosterone, while others are afraid of losing their hair. Some worry about being assaulted, or what God would think about it, or whether they would ever lose their hips. One person worries that after transition, he would be in an auto accident and upon 'discovery' he had a vagina, he would be buried as a 'she' with a dress, and news reports would be calling him a 'she.'

To give you a quick overview of *some* of the issues transmasculine individuals are fearful of losing when they make the decision to begin living authentically, here is a short list:

The loss of:
- respect from many medical providers
- recognition from government and state entities as your true gender
- being protected in employment
- being protected under the discrimination act and fears of being evicted
- spouses/partners/significant others
- parental support/siblings
- religious affiliations
- being recognized as part of the LGBT community
- dignity when aging and being placed in a care facility - if one will take you.
- the opportunity to admire a stranger's young child without being called a pedophile

- the loss of the ability to wear pink or pastels or carrying a handbag because of the fear of harassment

As serious and disheartening as the statistics and physical losses are, as well as the fears that precede and accompany these losses, there are other worries, too; to the individual facing these losses they are just as relevant and critical as the physical losses. These are the losses which involve their psychological well-being—the loss of their former selves, their self-identities, and their connections to the safety of women's spaces. To some, these losses are the determining factor on whether or not they choose to physically transition. I want to examine these specific losses and demonstrate just how crucial to a person's mental health and decision to transition might be.

Loss of Identity

I have written quite a bit on identities throughout Part I, yet I believe I may have missed an important slice of the pie—defining what I mean when I refer to *identities*. Perhaps the simplest and straight-forward definition is best suggested by Burke & Tully, (1977) —an identity is a set of 'meanings' applied to the self in a social role or situation defining what it means to be who one is. In viewing it in this way, *one's identity is who one is.* To make a choice to physically alter one's body with hormones or surgery or both, appears to completely shatter one's self-ideations up to that point.

Conflicts can arise when there may be a perceived negative connection between perceived conflicting identities within one's self. The increased congruence toward one identity decreases the congruence toward another identity, and the result is distress stemming from these inconsistencies (Burke, 1991). This in turn affects behaviors, emotions and overall self-image of the individual experiencing these apparent incompatibilities, creating fears, questions, and hesitations while deep down inside, the individual's authentic self is struggling to be recognized and released.

What many are not aware of is that once one becomes a 'he' rather than a 'she' (although there are those who reject the binary and choose they/them/theirs or other suitable pronouns for themselves), 'he' moves into a position of privilege, one that 'she' found oppressive. 'He' moves into a place of confidence, forgetting that 'she' could not walk alone in the dark because of other 'he's'.

If one is coming into his authenticity from the lesbian community, after taking the step and being perceived as a man, he is now focused even more acutely on the other inevitable, the thing that he feared most: He finds that his closest friends, the lesbian women and community to whom he has invested a significant portion of his life, those who pre-ferred the 'she'—promptly rejected him for his 'betrayal' of the feminine. His fears have come true, and it is a place of uncomfortableness. It is often a turning point in this individual's life—he can choose accept it and embrace his past experiences that made him the man he is today, or he can dismiss the past and reject those who rejected him, concentrating solely on being the man he is, refusing and rebuffing all things female for himself because they are no longer a part of his life, or so he chooses to believe. Often, and sadly, some of these men turn to dismissing or rejecting others who choose to remember and value their former lives, often with attitudes and words that can only be described as transmiso-gynistic, a term I wrote about in the previous chapter.

One of Henri Tajfel's (1979) main contributions to psychology was his Social Identity Theory which posits:

> *Social identity is a person's sense of who they are based on their group membership(s).*

Tajfel proposed that the groups (family, sports, associations, or other) which people belonged to were an important source of pride and self-esteem. Groups give us a sense of social identity—they give us a sense of belonging. We have divided the world into groups or categories, but in doing so, we have created "us" and "them," and we have worked to enhance or build up the "us" to diminish "them." We all can, and do, have many identities—parent, teacher, volunteer, therapist, artist, musi-cian, researcher, attorney, athlete, construction worker, a writer, a club leader—the list goes on. Each identity places us in a role, or position, in life and all combined make up who we are. For some, their identification within the LGBT community is a prominent and vital and even essential part of who they are.

For many who embraced the lesbian or the feminist communities, they shared a commonality with them that other groups did not, or could not, offer. They invested themselves to form strong, lasting bonds with the group's purpose or function, and found solidarity and camaraderie with others in the group. While within this societally marginalized group, they saw those outside the group, as "them," something to avoid or challenge if the "them" threatened "us" (even if it was a perceived threat). These individuals embodied the identity of *lesbian* or *feminist* or both, and wore the label(s) proudly. Their identity became *meaning* and *expectation*, and was the essential core component that crafted them into the strong women they were. The community was their refuge, a safe harbor, a haven.

I've heard the stories of these men countless times over the years; those embarking on a physical transition have very valid fears of losing their community, and many of those who did transition lost this very special connection. Calvin Neufeld, a trans speaker, activist, and writer addresses this fear,

> Like many trans men my identity is heavily invested in solidarity with women, with lesbians and queers at large, but I no longer have access to my former place of natural intimacy within those circles of belonging. It isn't enough to tempt me to continue living as a female imposter but it is enough to leave me mourning the loss of that connection (2008, para. 6).

Belonging

The sense of belonging is a powerful incentive to many who are contemplating a physical transition. Belonging means being accepted and valued, it means being a part of something greater—belonging to a greater community improves motivation, health and happiness (Hall, 2014). Belonging is a basic human need, (Maslow, 1954) and necessary for self-actualization. A sense of belonging means you are not alone, there are others who experience life as you do, and it is a need that everyone possesses. There are those who seek belonging by excluding others—in doing so they are seeking to belong to the group that does not belong, yet this idea of *not* belonging has been shown to cause pain and conflict, too.

Kate Bornstein is a well-known 'gender-transgressor,' and says that the social order can only see transgender and non-conforming individuals in the form of *no self* or *otherness*, (absence or no community). We as trans individuals (like any other human being), have a "need for a recognizable identity, and the need to belong to a group of people with a similar identity . . . [these] are driving forces in our culture, and nowhere is this more evident than in the areas of gender and sexuality" (1994, p. 4–5). She allies herself with others who are 'transgressively gendered' and states "That's how I see myself: I live pretty much without a gender, which paradoxically means I can do many genders" (1998, p.14). Not everyone can be like Bornstein, however. (As an aside, there are those who think that one Kate Bornstein is enough or even too much. I happen to believe the world would be a much nicer place to be if it were full of individuals just like Kate!)

Then there are those who are not 'transgressively gendered,' those who are or feel like they may be more 'binary'—more male or more female. There are those who have belonged to the lesbian community for a significant length of time—those who have embodied the identity, the values, and the strength of other lesbian women—fear the loss of this special connection when they face the reality of understanding their authentic gender, which is in direct contrast to what they have known up to this point.

There are many transmasculine individuals who have not *always* known they were male, despite what medical and psychological textbooks have led us to believe. Not all of those who "come out" as trans were always boys or men—some only knew they never quite "fit in," or they had experienced some type of body dysphoria but dismissing it as an anomaly, and some knew their thought processes were different than other women, but chose to think of themselves as simply 'unique.' They may or may not have deeply identified as a lesbian woman.

But for those that identified as part of the lesbian *community*, not only will they likely lose that community and the solidarity with these women they have come to love, they will have to reexamine their ideologies they have formed within the community, especially if their particular community has a strong feminist influence. Jamison Greene (2005) speaks of some of what I will call the 'mental processing' these men go through in acknowledging their trans-ness,

> I needed to combat the lesbian-feminist doctrine of male
> evil—that all men are bad—which I knew was wrong be-
> cause I had always had close friends who were male and
> good relationships with my father and brother. I saw that
> doctrine as hypocritical, too, because many lesbians ap-
> proved of masculine traits in women, but despised them

in men" (p. 23).

What a lot of people cannot understand or comprehend is the undercurrents which occur when a member of the lesbian community finds themselves in the situation of feeling the need to live authentically—perhaps even just discovering that they are indeed men, and not butch— there are some lesbians who hold much animosity, even hatred, towards trans men and become *gender vigilantes,* seeing these men as "treasonous deserters…. and [they are] commonly perceived and described in contemptuous stereotypes: unhealthy, deluded, self-hating, enslaved to patriarchal gender roles, sick, antifeminist, and self-mutilating" (Rubin, 1992, p. 477).

Can you pause for a moment and imagine? Think of yourself in a social group that is important to you, one that you look forward to being active with and you are dedicated to being a valuable member. Now imagine that group being the center of your entire existence, it is a sacred part of you and something to be almost worshipped for its significance and the profound effect it has had in your life. You cannot imagine *not being* a part of the group, can you? You would experience an acute loss, one that would make you question everything you believed while in that group. Now imagine that fear of loss, only now it is even greater, because the loss means you have lost your *identity* along with your role or position in the group. Your entire foundation has just crumbled. This is what is felt when some transmasculine individuals consider their options for living authentically as men. They know they will lose that fundamental identity of lesbian, and/or the unique and deep-seated membership in the group. Many fear, too, that their feminist standing will also be challenged –for men cannot be feminists, right? Wrong, but this issue is literally a matter of "he said, she said" and not one to delve into any more deeply with this book.

Not only do many of these individuals experience the loss of the lesbian community, they are often subjected to the verbal and psychological abuse thrown at them by these women who were once their dearest friends. Now they are in the position of being heterosexual men (the enemy) who still love and care for these women who were of such importance to them just weeks or months prior to their transitions, but with no reciprocation. Then worse, they suddenly find themselves appearing to be on the 'outside' of the entire LGBT community! They may find a group of other like-minded transmasculine individuals for companionship, but far too many go through these life-crises alone. They have no one to turn to because they are suddenly the "straight" guy who seems to be infiltrating the gay and lesbian communities. They are seen as predators, and women cross the street to avoid them at night. Children look away and run behind their mothers because now you are the strange man about whom they have been warned.

Now they face not only the loss of community, they are also in a position where they might well be mourning the loss of their female self, for many reasons. However, they may have difficulty acknowledging this grief, because in doing so, it might pose a threat to their masculinity or in their decision to transition—they might believe that grieving would appear as regret or a lack of conviction.

Whether or not one has left the lesbian community or some other close connection who might be unaccepting of the change, or even if they were leaving a life of depression and lack of belonging, the "physical transition, while a welcomed change, means leaving behind the only life [they have] ever known, as painful as that life might have been" (Hansbury, 2005, p. 29, edits mine).

Facing the Fears

For those who have been considering a physical transition, or even just "coming out" as a trans or gender non-conforming person, they have been living in isolation, hiding and holding in their secrets. They are likely depressed and anxious, and full of many of the fears of loss that I mentioned previously. There can also be anxiety over many additional areas once one begins the process of physical transition;

- Frustrations of having to change or explain legal documents (driver's license, passport, titles to property, diplomas, birth certificate, and more)
- Fears about having to experience surgeries, and the effects of testosterone
- Anxiety about whether one will be satisfied with their appearance after hormones or surgery

Pursing a physical transition is not the proverbial 'cake walk.' All of the fears and anxieties are valid, with some of them worth careful consideration, such as the experiences with discrimination which could lead to violence. One must also weigh in whether or not they are willing to lose their family members or close friends due to their unwillingness to accept your authenticity. Fearing a job loss or housing situation, although not as emotionally devastating as losing loved one, are still very valid concerns.

There are no easy answers, and no one can answer the questions for someone else. If you are in this situation of wondering whether you should pursue a physical transition through hormones and even surgery, I can only say to first acknowledge your fears, but try not to feed them. Ask yourself which of your personal fears are truly valid fears that are holding you back—if it is the fear of going bald, is that serious enough for you to continue living in the way you have done up until now? If it is the fear of losing your family or friends, then you will need to ask yourself "What would the rest of my life be like if I don't transition?" Are you able to go on the way you have been? Be realistic in your thought processes. Ask yourself what are the real risks?

Put your risks—your fears—on a mental scale, or even write them on paper; does your perception of the risk of 100 on a scale of 0 to 100, meaning the event or situation will inevitably happen? At the other end of the scale, there is a zero risk that the fear might come true. All of them will certainly fall along the continuum, but if you weight them all in, being completely honest with yourself, you should have your answer and know in your heart what you need to do. And if it means not going through with a transition at this time, there is nothing that says you cannot revisit your fears at a later date and reconsider your options.

※※※

As I near the end of this last topic, I want to leave you with a passage that Griffin Hansbury (2002) wrote; a man who has experience with transition, who originally identified "as a feminist and as a dyke", and who now spends his life helping others of all genders in the Rainbow spectrum in his private practice. He puts the aspect of transition into perspective when he writes;

> Transition, the passage from one state to another, always involves gains and losses. Optimally, the gains outweigh the losses. Yet, even when what gets lost is given up gladly, the loss demands mourning. This is evident in normal life transitions, such as the movement from childhood to adolescence, young adulthood to middle-

> age, and so on, as well as in everyday rites of passage, like graduating high school, starting a new job, getting married, and having children. Every transition is, in some way, a kind of death (p. 22).

Lastly, I acknowledge the pain, the grief, the loss and the fears that are felt by so many in our community. I would like to be able to say everything will be all right, but until society, *including* this small community of ours inside of the wider population, experiences a major shift in perception, expectations and behaviors, it is highly probable that others will continue to experience what most of us have gone through to get to where we are now. It is not within the scope of this book to provide therapy or solutions to coping with these fears and losses, but instead it is meant to highlight the necessity of *understanding* these occurrences— these deep emotional experiences—so that perhaps, someday, we will begin to see changes that promise an end to discrimination and a light at the end of what has been a centuries old tunnel of inequalities and inequities.

8

Seque

As I now approach the end of Part I, I ask that you keep in mind all that you have read up to this point as you continue into Part II of this book. You will find the stories of transmasculine individuals who, because of this book, have had the opportunity to find their voices and share their truths. You will find facets of their personal stories that reflect on issues covered here in Part I. With gender politics, correctness, and discrimination aside and ignored, these individuals communicate their experiences and realities in the hopes of opening hearts and minds to this wonderful world of diversity we experience here in the transmasculine community.

I would like to leave you with one parting thought. These words of Bornstein (1994) reflect the dream of nearly every trans individual—man, woman, and all those in-between and around with their fluidly-gendered lives—and one day, there may be enough voices to make this dream a reality.

> And you—you still think gender is the issue! Gender is not the issue. Gender is the battlefield. Or the playground. The issue is us versus them. Any us versus any them. One day we may not need that (p. 222).

❀❀❀ End Part I ❀❀❀

PART II

Embodiment of Diversity

It is through self-narrative that persons give meaning to their experiences and achieve a sense of their lives unfolding; it is through narrative that persons structure their lived experience into sequences of events in time—through past, present and future—and according to certain plots. These personal narratives are not reflections of lives as they are lived, but narratives that are actually constitutive of life; they are not stories about life, but stories that have real effects in the shaping of lives and of relationships. ~ (M. White, 1996, p. 176)

The Contributors: Who Are They?

I have chosen to step outside the box with where to locate this section about the Contributors because I know many people don't actually go to the end to read about each one, and many people skip the pages at the beginning of a book. Including it here at the beginning of Part II seems appropriate, and it is more likely that you will read about them to learn more about who they are.

Without the stories of the following individuals, this book would be just another "educational" book. Combining these individual's personal stories here in Part II, with the "education" in Part I, the topics become more personal and real. As you read through their personal narratives, you will find a wide variety of backgrounds and experiences, but remember that all of these individuals have at least two things in common: They each have *herstory* they are proud to share with you, and each of them are living their truth.

※※※

Maxwell Alderdice lives in a suburb of Seattle, Washington, with a small black and white cat and a lot of big colorful ideas. He is currently drafting a novel for the purpose of exploring his experiences as a transgender man through speculative fiction.

Bobbi Aubin is a 51-year-old Transgender Male, single parent to one, and who works for Laurentian University in the Aboriginal Student Affairs Office. Bobbi would have loved to start transitioning at the age of five; however, there were no words in the 1960s to describe what he was experiencing. It was not until his mid-forties when he stumbled upon the language of Transgender, that he began his journey to become the man he is today.

Avi Ben-Zeev, Ph.D. is a Jewish Middle Eastern gay transgender man and a professor of psychology at San Francisco State University (SFSU), where he directs the Cognition and Social Equity lab and is the Co-Coordinator of the Mind, Brain & Behavior Program. He received his Ph.D. in Cognitive Psychology from Yale University in 1997. Dr. Ben-Zeev serves as a multiple PI on SF BUILD, a large-scale project funded by a grant from the National Institutes of Health (NIH) for creating institutional change that promotes multiculturalism while recognizing and overcoming the effects of implicit bias and stereotype threat. Dr. Ben-Zeev has been serving on the editorial boards of Psychology of Popular Media Culture and the Journal of Homosexuality and has authored high impact publications in top-tier journals, such as Psychological Science, Journal of Experimental Social Psychology and Cognitive Science. Dr. Ben-Zeev has also edited and co-authored books on cognition published by Lawrence Erlbaum and Oxford University Press.

Cooper Lee Bombardier, MS, MFA is a writer and visual artist based in Portland, Oregon. His work appears in many publications and anthologies, most recently in CutBank, Nailed Magazine, Original Plumbing, and is forthcoming in The Kenyon Review and MATRIX, as well as the anthology The Remedy–Essays on Queer Health Issues, (ed. Zena Sharman) from Arsenal Pulp Press. He started out teaching writing through WritersCorps in San Francisco two decades ago, and currently teaches writing at Portland State University, the University of Portland, at Grant High School through Writers in The Schools, and online at LitReactor. Learn more at at www.cooperleebombardier.com

Lee Harrington is an internationally known sexuality and spirituality educator, gender explorer, eclectic artist and award-winning author and editor on human erotic and sacred experience. He's been traveling the globe (Seattle to Sydney, Berlin to Boston), teaching and talking about sexuality, psychology, faith and desire, and believes you deserve passion and connection in your life. His books include "Traversing Gender: Understanding Transgender Journeys," "Sacred Kink: The Eightfold Paths of BDSM and Beyond," and "Shibari You Can Use: Japanese Rope

Bondage and Erotic Macramé," among many others. Lee has been a passion instigator, academic, adult film performer, world class sexual adventurer, outspoken philosopher, kink/bondage expert, and has been blogging about sex and spirit since 1998. Read more about Lee at PassionAndSoul.com.

L.W. Lucas Hasten lives in the San Francisco Bay area where he has been teaching anthropology to community college students since 2001. Having spent his entire adult life as a proud butch lesbian, it came as a surprise to almost no one when he came out as transgender last year at the age of 49. Within six months of beginning hormone therapy, a mustache made its appearance which granted him the convenience of passing. His feminist soul winces at the sudden onslaught of white male privilege, which he tries to offset by being a vocal advocate for women and people of color. You can find him online at lwhasten.com, which has links to his blog, his podcasts, and his semi-professional landscape photography.

Jackson Jantzen spent 20 years deeply rooted in the lesbian community before coming to terms with his relationship to gender identity in his late 30s. His partner of 14 years, Julia, supported and partnered with him as embraced his gender identity and took steps to live more authentically in the world. He currently serves as the Executive Director of The Center: 7 Rivers LGBTQ Connection, an LGBTQ+ resource center serving 11 rural counties in the Midwest region of the United States.

Tygh Lawrence-Clarke is a 51 year old transman. He was born in Beverly Hills, CA and was raised by a single mother, who was a prominent physician. His family moved to Las Vegas when he was 11, where he remained for most of his life. He retired in 2011 from the Pharmacy field to become a stay at home Dad. He now lives in the woods of New Hampshire with his wife, son and his menagerie of pets. Since his transition, Tygh now spends his free time advocating for the transgender community. He has a Youtube channel where he documents his transition and makes educational videos. He, with the help of his wife, is also working with a nonprofit organization called 41Percent, which strives to pair people in the transgender community with supportive volunteer peers, in an effort to address the suicide problem. Despite the challenges Tygh faces every day, he couldn't be happier now that he is living his life as his true self.

Shawn L. owns a small music business in rural Maryland where he re-sides with his partner of almost 19 years and two beautiful four legged children. He enjoys building and flying model airplanes, studying the history of WWII and enjoying the outdoors. He runs a blog on Word-press titled Dawn to Don, Trans-Formation at Midlife, which discusses his transition and feelings about being transgender. His blog can be found at lesboi.wordpress.com.

Max Meyer is a 23-year-old transman. He studies agriculture and hopes to combine his passion for sustainability and writing. He helped to create the first registered group for trans* students on his university campus, and he finds solidarity in sharing his transition experience.

Stephen Ostrow is a Licensed Massage Therapist, Bodyworker and Yoga Guide in persuit of a MA in Somatic Psychology. They identify as non-binary and trans-masculine. Their goal is to share their body posi-tive & identity fluid process and practice with the world. In the past, they have sat on numerous community information panels about trans issues and co-facilitated workshops about how to support trans and non-binary identities. They are always open to sharing their story, edu-cating others about the diverse spectrum of gendered experiences, and the many accompanying issues that exist and must be overcome. Ste-phen is also an engaged member of a meditation community and helped cultivate and co-facilitated Queer Dharma groups. You can learn more or contact them via yogiostrow.wordpress.com.

Evan R. began his journey of transition to his authentic self in Novem-ber 2011, and has chosen to live his live quietly, away from the trans community, and prefers being seen as a male in society. He lived as a lesbian for 38 years and experienced discrimination, but his transition was relatively easy, leaving the discrimination behind. He enjoys spend-ing time with his trans friends and acquaintances, and he shares his story with others in various ways in hopes of helping others along in their transition journeys. He and his girlfriend are engaged to be married, and he works as a landscaper/farmer while they look for land where they can build an off-grid homestead together

Caden Rocker was raised primarily in a small town in Upstate New York, other than for a few years living in Maine as a young child. He lived as a cisgender female for about the first 20 years of his life, coming out as a lesbian in his freshmen year in High School. In school, he was the first openly out person with others following after him, and he continued to be out and in the open until graduating high school in 2001. After graduation, and as soon as he was able, he moved away from the town he grew up in and spent time living in Vermont, Arizona. He currently lives in Albuquerque, NM. After working in the food-service industry for over 15 years, he returned to college, and is currently working with different non-profits that mainly deal with issues concerning LGBTQ individuals. He also enjoy spending time outdoors and photography.

Tristan Rounkles is a dreamer, creator, knowledge-seeker, fighter, and hopeless romantic. He lives in an urban area, in a city that has made him feel at home. His life is shared with a wonderful, loving, supportive partner as well as two sweet pups. He currently works as a sales assistant for a company that manufactures natural pet products. His future career goals include professional writing and editing. He would like to start his own business when the time is right. He is content with the present, but looks forward to his future.

Hunter T. made his transition late in life. Prior to transition, Hunter played along in the lesbian world, identifying as a butch dyke who was most comfortable on the softball field. A US Navy veteran, Hunter is a writer, photographer and a craftsman, who resides in Seattle, WA. He is currently working on his website to help other transmen adjust to a new life, specifically men who transition later in life.

Day Walker was born in 1965 and raised in the Oakland Bay Area, California, Day identifies as Agender and is happily married to their wife of 12 years. Day is educated in Behavioral Sciences - although they spent over 25 years in the Motorcycle Industry. Day has been described as a modern day philosopher and a Hippy who loves to hug trees and whispers to Crows. Day is an Author, an Artist, an occasional Poet and a Mentor to many. They now reside in the Mountains of Southern Humboldt County where they continue to hug trees and whisper to all creatures that will listen.

Lucas Aiden Wehle is a trans man who has dedicated his life to social justice advocacy. In the 5 years since he transitioned, Lucas has lectured, mentored, facilitated workshop, lead support/discussion groups and has been a vocal advocate for LGBTQIA issues. For Lucas, "no one wins unless we all do". He now works at Metro Wellness as their Trans & Youth Program Coordinator. In addition to his professional career, he volunteers as a member of the board of directors for PFLAG Tampa. Most importantly, his cat Shark thinks he is pretty awesome.

10

My Journey: Trans Boy to Lesbian to Trans Butch

By Shawn L.
Age 54, Transmasculine Butch

[Editor Note: Like many who have come from lesbian back-grounds, Shawn has experienced the loss of that community, some-thing you read about in Chapter 7; he also realizes and accepts those experiences, because they will always be a part of his life. He embraces his past, his 'herstory', because it made him into the per-son he is today. You'll read here first-hand his contemplations and experiences as he continued to follow his journey to the present.]

❧❧❧

It took me a long time to fully understand myself and it wasn't until my mid-forties that I started to realize that I was actually transgender and not the dyke lesbian I had thought I was since the 1980s. But once I made that connection and really understood it, so many things became clearer and made much more sense to me.

From my earliest memories as a child, being a girl seemed like a tiny little confining box that suffocated me. I was only happy when I was allowed to explore outside of that box and be the boy that I was. Looking back now, I can clearly see that I had a boyhood up until I hit puberty. I played war, cowboys and Indians, went fishing with my male cousins, played with toy soldiers on rainy days and was, in general, a typical little boy. Yet, I was told that I was a tomboy and that my interest in all this "boy stuff" would fade away as I got older. It never did. The grown-ups were wrong. It's just that none of us knew it for a really long time.

Eventually, I did stop playing with toy guns and started being interested in girls, not as friends, but like the other boys were interested in them. And the boys were no longer safe to hang out with and didn't have any interest in me as a pal anymore. They were starting to see me as I saw girls and that scared the hell out of me. At the same time, though, I was getting a very clear message from my mother and the rest of the world that I was expected to be interested in boys sexually. I wasn't at all interested in them that way, but I felt like I needed to try and pretend like I was. Inside my head, I developed a very vivid fantasy world where I was a boy/man and the girls I was crushing on were my girlfriends. My fantasy world helped me cope with my feelings, but I didn't understand it until many years later.

While I was crushing on girls and pretending to like boys, I was developing some strong friendships with several girls who would become lifelong friends. Thinking back on it now, I'm really amazed that I was able to deal with the complicated relationship I had with these ladies. I would crush on one of them for a while, and one in particular pretty constantly throughout high school. At the same time, we were just friends having sleep overs, slumber parties and partying together. I listened to them talk about their boyfriends or crushes while struggling with the jealousy I felt inside. I wanted them to crush on me but I never dared to tell any of them how I felt and I certainly never acted on my feelings either. It was my deep dark secret that I dared not speak of to anyone. To me, I was just weird. None of it made any sense to me, but I kept myself too busy to give it much thought.

College years came along and one of my roommates became my first sexual encounter. She told me I was a lesbian, which I had very little understanding of. So, from then on I believed I was a lesbian. I was freaked out, ashamed and scared but at the same time felt like this must be the answer to why I was so weird. Interestingly, even though I was consistently in lesbian relationships from that point on, my fantasies of being a man in a straight relationship continued. It didn't make any sense to me. I was finally able to express my attraction to women, yet I still felt this need to fantasize. It was a mystery that finally was answered once I realized I was really transgender.

I moved from the east coast of the U.S. to Chicago, IL in 1985 to pursue a master's degree. I wanted to get away from my mother, who had figured out my lesbian "lifestyle" and was making life very difficult for me. Chicago was a fantastic place for me to spread my wings as a lesbian. There was a rich scene going on there with lots of bars, coffee houses, support groups, other women, etc. to keep my young baby butch self-entertained and happy. I was introduced to "women's music" at this time by a friend I met in my dorm. I don't remember the name of the artist but she gave me a cassette tape to listen to of a lesbian folk singer. I listened to that tape nonstop and wanted to hear more. I was in awe to discover we had our own newspaper and that became my lifeline for what was going on in the city. I discovered the Mountain Moving Coffeehouse which was a womyn-only space, operated on a sliding scale for admittance, and put on women's music concerts every Saturday evening. I went there a lot! I heard some awesome music and really thrived on the amazing energy from the other womyn. I heard a lot of the popular women performers of the day there and bought their albums.

During this time, I had a girlfriend that I had met at a Labor Day picnic held by a group called *Kinheart*, consisting of two women who held support groups and classes on coming out. My girlfriend told me she wanted to go to this women's music festival in Michigan that summer and wanted me to go with her. It would be fun, she said. You camp on the womyn-only land with all the other womyn, go to interesting workshops on all these different topics during the day, buy cool stuff from the female artisans and listen to amazing women's music at night under the stars of the August sky. Sure, why not? It sounded like fun. Well, we got there, and the first thing I saw were naked women running around directing traffic and telling us where to go. I freaked out a bit because I wasn't prepared for being naked in the woods with a bunch of strangers, but I quickly learned that clothing was optional and I relaxed.

The experience of attending the Michigan Womyn's Music Festival was life changing for me. It was akin to a spiritual awakening, a celebration of the feminine, a religious experience of sorts and a wonderful break from everyday life where I couldn't be public about my sexuality. Listening to the music at night under the stars, watching shooting stars cross the sky, was magical. Watching "*Desert Hearts*" with thousands of other lesbians before it was even out in the theaters was the icing on the cake.

I left Michigan forever touched by the magic there and vowed to go back. I did go back once a couple of years later by myself. Again, it was a great experience and one that I always hoped to have again. I was saddened to hear that the festival closed last year. It was like going to lesbian boot camp or a crash course on all things lesbian. I learned so much about what it is to be a lesbian, and a womyn, there. I carry a vast amount of gratitude that I got to experience something so special.

From Chicago, I moved to the Minneapolis/St. Paul area of Minnesota with my partner at that time. It was a much different scene and it took me a long time to adjust to it. The bars and coffeehouses were replaced by camping trips and softball games. I became part of a group of women who became like family to me. To me, they were my family. My own family was not supportive of who I was, but with these women I could just be myself. I feel, in a way, that these women "raised" me. One woman in particular was sort of the mom of the group. We often spent holidays at her house eating her delicious homemade food. It was a very nurturing and fun environment of playing games and hanging out. This, to me, is what family life should be like.

Eventually, I felt the need to return to my home state and reclaim my right to be there and live my life on my own terms so I left my little family in Minnesota and struck out on my own. It was one of the hardest things I ever did, but I felt like I had to do it. I never have had the amazing lesbian experiences of Chicago or the tight knit lesbian family of Minnesota again, and my life as a lesbian really became just an ordinary life of building a career and a life with my present partner for the past 18 years. We occasionally go up to the city for a Pride festival or to a Melissa Etheridge concert, but mostly we live our ordinary lives in the country.

I look back now at all of my rich experiences of my young adult days and feel a lot of different emotions. I had no idea what being transgender meant back then. All I knew was that I was attracted to women, and I was a woman, so I was a lesbian. It was pretty simple in my mind. It's been pointed out to me that my lesbian herstory sheltered me from understanding the truth about myself sooner. Perhaps. Maybe it also sheltered me from crippling dysphoria that, in the 1980s and early 90s, would have been extremely traumatic and difficult to do anything about. Maybe it made it a lot more tolerable to be a masculine/male identified person in a female body. It was okay for me to be masculine. Those lesbians celebrated my butch qualities. In fact, I was, by far, not the butchest of the butches. And my love for music was a tonic to my soul as I grew and learned about myself back in those days.

We all have our own paths to follow and we get where we're going when we're ready. I couldn't have handled knowing I was transgender at 18. I'm thankful for my lesbian herstory and mourn the loss of no longer being welcome in womyn-only spaces. Handing in my "lesbian card" to gain my "transman card" is tough. Yet, I don't feel like the two things can't co-exist within me. I'm a trans man with a lesbian herstory and I self-identify as a transmasculine butch dude. My lesbian past has helped to shape me into the man I am today. It's been an amazing journey to find myself and to understand how this puzzle that is me all fits together. I'm so thankful for the experiences I've had and the understanding I've gained through realizing that I'm actually transgender.

11

Beshert* a Yiddish expression for something that was "meant to be"

By L.W. Lucas Hasten
Age 50, Man

[Editor Note: Lucas brings the painful realities of his life before transition into a form we can all understand, and more than a few might even empathize with his particular struggles. We all come to the place of having to look deep within ourselves in order to find our way out of ourselves. This story illustrates this process by capturing the reader's emotions in order to really understand his struggles, and giving us a glimpse of the reality of living in a body that doesn't reflect who we are.]

✿✿✿

I remember laying on the floor of the dressing room with my head tucked under my arms, heaving with sobs, breathing fast and shallow. The tiny room spun around me. The pants were only partway up, too small to make it past my hips. I don't know how long I was there like that, silently hyperventilating. Eventually I managed to collect myself and leave, buying the only pair that zipped all the way up. They would have to do.

I'd been asked to sit on an interview committee for candidates for a new position at the College, a job that called for "professional attire."

Living life as I do, in jeans and an assortment of colored polo shirts, it meant I'd have to go shopping. I hit the local mall. I began in what I refer to as "the fat ladies section," hoping desperately that Ralph Lauren had seen fit to put out a pair of tailored pants for the season.

Entering the women's department, I felt the same mixture of nausea and resentment I've known since childhood, a wave of anger at whomever it was that decided women should wear these clothes. I joked (without humor) that I might one day hang myself right there in the women's department at Macy's with a note that says, "If you want to know why, just look around."

As I moved through the racks, I was met with confused looks. I'm sure people were wondering what a man was doing there alone, rifling through women's clothing. The shape of my body left me little choice in the matter; while I hated the style of women's clothes, men's clothes didn't fit right. I'd resigned myself long ago to wearing jeans exclusively. There's something magically androgynous about denim.

The women's section held nothing I was willing to wear, so I gave up and crossed the store to the men's department. Whatever I might find there would fit poorly, but at least I'd like it. When I was a child and no one was home, I'd dress up in my father's shirts and ties. I figured out how to tie a four-in-hand knot, having watched him do it often enough. Looking in the mirror, I'd visualize myself as a handsome and gallant provider, the kind of man who opens doors and pulls out chairs for women: Cary Grant, Jimmy Stewart, Gregory Peck.

I walked past the rows of ties and pocket squares, yearning. While I loved them, I'd always felt that neckties were a step too far. My butch persona was off-putting enough to strangers; a tie would be even more in-your-face. It felt aggressive; like grabbing onto a sign of status to which I wasn't entitled and yelling at everybody about it. I headed straight for the pants.

Praying I'd make it into the largest size they carried, I gathered an armload of size 44s and hesitated. Should I use the men's fitting room? That would be awkward with breasts and a fat ass. Sighing deeply, I headed back across the store to the women's department. If you've ever shopped at Macy's, then you know there is almost never an attendant at the fitting room. Why then, was there someone standing at the entrance that day, watching me as I approached? "*Beshert*," my sister would say: It was meant to be. The woman smiled at me kindly and pointed in the opposite direction. "The men's fitting room is that way."

My face reddened. I stuck out my chest and eyed it obviously. "I'm a

Beshert* a Yiddish expression for something that was "meant to be"

woman," I said, and the attendant, horrified by her own mistake, apologized. I made my way to a dressing room in the back and hung up the pants. I'd chosen six pairs.

I kicked off my shoes and sighed again, the dread overtaking me. None of these will fit me. I'll be lucky if I find a single pair that zips. What the hell am I doing here? Why do I feel like an alien on the planet? What am I going to do? What am I going to wear? I hate my body. I hate dealing with it. I hate looking at it. I hate being in it. I'm too old for this. It's just getting worse. I'm going to die like this.

Somehow I made my way through five pairs before the last one brought me down. I'm not sure how long it lasted, me laying on the floor like that, overcome with grief and anxiety. When it stopped, I pulled myself together quickly and paid my bill in silence.

That's the moment I stopped eating. Not completely, because I wasn't quite settled on dying, but little enough food to indicate that I was pretty much done with living. I was forty-nine years old which, from the perspective of prehistory, is a long life, and I'd had enough. I was exhausted. Proud of my work as a teacher and the things I'd be leaving behind, I was finished. I felt like fading away.

Weeks went by. I went to work, I did my job, and I came home to my wife. I said nothing. It was clear to her that I had no appetite, but she had no idea why. In moments alone I asked myself: What is the core of this pain? (I hate my body.) Why am I sick to my stomach? (I'm nauseous with anxiety because something big is coming.) Why do I hate my body so much? (Because I'm fat.) Is it just because I'm overweight? (No.) What is it then? (My body doesn't match my mind.) But my body is perfectly healthy. (I must be out of my mind.)

I've held this core belief, that there is something very deeply wrong with me, since I was four years old. Descending from my bedroom on a hot summer day in nothing but shorts, I was immediately sent back to retrieve an undershirt. "But Dad isn't wearing one," I protested, "so why do I have to?"

"Because he's a boy and you're a girl. Now go upstairs and get a shirt."

"Oh," I said mostly to myself as every cell in my body deflated.

Despite my mother's assertion, there's always been something about me that makes people read me as male. Throughout my childhood, adult strangers referred to me as "son," and "young man," regardless of the length of my hair. It was the '70s, after all. And aside from the year I turned thirteen, when Bar- or Bat-Mitzvah attendance required wearing a dress, I never wore anything remotely feminine.

Boys weren't interested in me. I was into reading, music, and intense friendships with other girls. I once talked a friend into a "you-show-me-yours-and-I'll-show-you-mine" situation where I chickened out after she showed me hers. I'd intended to show at first, but in the end my embarrassment kept me from revealing a body somehow wrong.

I turned twenty-one without ever dating anyone and then I joined a rock band. It was three years of self-abuse in girl drag, including the occasional hetero hook-up. More than once, I hurriedly left the scene at an unacceptable midpoint between nudity and penetration. At twenty-three I accepted the fact that I was exclusively attracted to women and came out as a lesbian. A couple of years later I realized "butch" summed it up and took ownership of that label.

When I attended graduate school in my early thirties, I studied gender and sexuality across cultures. On some level, I was looking for validation. I did my Master's thesis on a group of drag kings – women who performed dressed as men – in New York City in the late '90s. I spent about a year doing interviews and attending events, ostensibly studying the culture but internally examining myself.

With the exception of one person, all of my informants thought of themselves as entertainers who were solidly female identified. Drag was a performance, not an identity. It was focused on camp and satire, distinctly feminist and lesbian in tone. The penis was a ridiculous object of derision and over-emphasis, and masculinity was not admired.

I was surprised then, when I moved to the San Francisco Bay area a few years later, to discover a drag king culture quite different, where many people used drag as an intermediate step toward transitioning to male. The whole FTM phenomenon was much bigger on the West coast than it had been in New York. There seemed to be a large network of support for it here.

An old friend of mine transitioned from female to male after moving to the Bay area but de-transitioned a few years later. When I asked her why, she explained that she felt like a faker when people gendered her male. She couldn't own the identity. She said she had transitioned for the wrong reasons; in part, to please a partner. She longed for her previous expression of femininity. I formed a hypothesis: Some people transition because they feel more support for that identity than their current one. This allowed me to fool myself for another ten years.

I stayed away from clothing stores. I didn't have to think about my body as long as I avoided highly gendered spaces. I had regular trouble in restrooms and locker rooms, where women occasionally accused me

Beshert* a Yiddish expression for something that was "meant to be"

of being a man, so I tried to keep out of those too. My wife took to accompanying me to the bathroom whenever we were out in public, just so I wouldn't be harassed by other women.

After the Macy's episode (I always italicize this in my mind), I started watching YouTube videos; they may have saved my life. By far, the vast majority of FTM videos posted were by very young guys, and while I had a hard time identifying with them, they let me know that transitioning had become socially acceptable. Eventually I found one older transman – "Electric Dade" – with a supportive wife and a new baby who gave me hope for myself.

Subsisting on coffee and the occasional protein bar, I lost fifteen pounds in the three weeks it took me to decide that I could keep on living. As soon as I saw the path forward, an internal force propelled me into calling or meeting with everyone important in my life immediately to come out as transgender. I ate my first full meal upon completing the final conversation with my closest friends.

Reactions were uniform. My wife's words were telling: "I knew that when I met you." The friend I've known since childhood reminded me that I'd gendered us both male in a story I'd written forty years earlier. Another friend, made much more recently, said she'd been wondering why I *wasn't* transgender, since my male identification was so obvious. My sister she said she finally understood why I was always so miserable despite having a loving partner and a successful career. I hadn't realized it was that apparent.

As soon as my appetite returned, I started eating right to lose weight. Heart disease runs in my family and testosterone will cause whatever fat is sitting on my hips and ass to migrate to my gut, where it will increase my risk of heart attack. There's no way I'm letting that happen after waiting so long for this.

I'm less than a year into it, but my life changed the day I committed to transitioning. Hope and anticipation dropped into my psyche, replacing a lifetime of resignation. A lightness of being shines in my eyes, motivating a newly present smile. I stand half an inch taller since having my top surgery, done with hunching and hiding. My shoulders are growing broader if only because I'm holding them back now, my head no longer habitually bent in sadness. I walk through the world differently.

Frequently gendered as male before I began testosterone, a tidy little mustache showed up within six months, granting me the privilege of passing. For the first time in my life, I love what I see in the mirror. The fat has been burning, not shifting, and my ass has evaporated. I'm starting to look like the guy I've always seen in my head. I'm finally becoming the man I thought I'd never get to be.

Do you want to know what my favorite thing to do is now? Meet me at Macy's.

12

A Strong Feminist Voice

By Bobbi Aubin
Age 51, Trans Male

[*Editor Note: Bobbi's story is like so many others, in that when he was a youth in the 1960s, finding the language and terminology to describe what he felt when the term transgender had yet become known, and transsexual was not something for a youth to consider. He applied himself fully to everything he committed to do until it no longer worked for him, and the truth of who he was stayed with him until he found the right language for which he had been searching. As you read his story, you will see a man who learned from it all, and draws upon his past to help enlighten others in hopes for a brighter future.*]

❧❧❧

My name is Bobbi Aubin and I am 51 years old. Since the age of five, I have been at odds with who I am. I was told at a very young age that I could not be a boy, and was forever put into dresses and forced to play with dolls. I preferred "borrowing" my brothers' trucks/cars to play with. I had cut all the hair off my doll and had "tattooed" its entire body with pens. I had long, thick black hair, which, for the most part, was kept in braids. I found out that if I slept with gum in my mouth, it would eventually find its way into my long mane and Mom would have to cut it out, and eventually she was forced to cut it all off. THAT made me happy!

My childhood turned out okay for the most part, in that once home from school, the dress would be replaced with shorts or pants and in warmer months, I could get away with no shirt, which enabled freedom from playing the girl part. Until I started puberty that is. Then, I was forced to wear a, *ugh*, bra which turned me into a rebel and recluse. I would wear my brother's clothes whenever I could until he complained he had no clean clothes to wear. I finished Grades 7 and 8 wearing my brother's leisure suit. I really wanted to be a boy; however, I had no words to describe my feelings, I could only show it on the outside, physically.

From a very young age, I was made to see the difference between being female and male. I thought I was a boy until age five, when my oldest brother showed me I was made differently than him. He took advantage of my femaleness from my tender age of five until I turned twenty-one.

In 1984, my father introduced me to a man who eventually became my husband. We were happy hunting and fishing, but when it came to intimacy, I was not present emotionally. We married and two years later had a child. His fishing buddies would tease him about our lack of "love-making" and I became even more miserable. I hated the fact that he would tell his friends about our intimacy problems, and I truly was not a happy camper. I stayed in the relationship for my daughter's sake.

Fourteen years into our union, my past started to resurface. I refused to lie beside him, and he began to drink heavily. That is when I talked to him about my past, when he was drunk. It felt safe because he didn't remember anything the next day. It got so bad that I thought about suicide, every day. The day before I finally left, I had a gun in my mouth and was about to pull the trigger when I thought about my daughter. I didn't want her to grow up the way I did. I wrote Michael a letter and left that day with my daughter.

We moved to Sudbury, Ontario where I began my healing from my past journey. I met several women from the community who helped me find support with Women's shelters and a Sexual Assault Crisis Centre. This enabled me to relive my past in a safe and non-judgmental way. It was then that I discovered Lesbianism. It was truly a shock to be welcomed into a community that I shunned and always followed the crowd in homophobia. I had found myself. I met so many other women like me and was finally comfortable in my own skin. The slacks and blouses were replaced with Docs, Levi's and t-shirts from the men's section at Value Village. I learned the different lingo in terms of identifying as

Lesbian. I was a Butch Dyke and so proud of it.

I enrolled in College, received 3 diplomas from 3 different programs, same disciplines, all related to children and youth and became an Activist in Women's' Rights. I became a Feminist! I was the one whom they gave the loudspeaker to at Take Back The Night Marches! I had a VOICE and was not afraid to use it! The little wallflower I once was now bloomed and became larger than life! I had started Wen-Do classes, self-defense classes for women and girls and I became a leader in the classes because of all of the anger that was pent up in me. Again, I found a voice I did not know was possible! I encouraged women and girls to fight back, and not take any shit from anybody....

I identified as a Dyke for about 13 years, until I started to meet and hear about Transgender folk. I was in awe. Here I was meeting people who I would have never known were born of the opposite gender! I started to inquire about Trans folk. I did research and realized *this is me*! This is what I have felt like my entire life! I had finally found the language I never knew existed. I spoke to my daughter about it and her response was "whatever makes you happy, Mom."

I started my journey as a Transman in 2010. I found the organization I needed to connect with in Toronto Ontario at the Gender Identity Clinic with Centre for Addiction and Mental Health (CAMH). I had to live as a man for one whole year before I could be diagnosed with Gender Dysphoria. It felt like a very long process; however, every time I look back now, I can see that it was not. I have had a total hysterectomy, top surgery and am now waiting to hear if I get coverage for bottom surgery.

I am still a feminist today, a male feminist. A male feminist who has given birth. A male feminist with a vagina. A male feminist who advocates for women's rights.

I work in a University with Aboriginal students. I had a very macho, male colleague who would try and "teach" me how to be a man. He no longer works here. I often get invited into classrooms to talk about my life, and my transition and the fact that I am a feminist. It really warms my heart when skeptical students come full circle once my talk is done and ask questions, that's when I know I am making a difference in this little corner of the world.

13

The Love That Remains

By Cooper Lee Bombardier
Age 46, Queer/Transman/Butch

[*Editor Note: The feeling of being unseen, of being an outsider to a community once called home…to find out one is to be avoided, because of crossing an invisible border. Cooper attempts to put a name to the feelings of the loss, yet the words he finds aren't as all-encompassing as the sensations. The memories of the early years are not to be regretted, however, but instead remembered fondly—they were a welcoming place, a place he belonged—a life he can look back on and embrace because he is no longer bound to it.*]

✣✣✣

I always used to dream of the past
But like they say yesterday never comes
Sometimes there's a song in my brain
And I feel that my heart knows the refrain
I guess it's just the music that brings on nostalgia
For an age yet to come"
Buzzcocks – "Nostalgia"

I listen to my friend B talk about her obsession with the dyke culture of 1990s San Francisco, something I was part of and she was not. She wonders aloud if there is a word that describes a sense of nostalgia for a time in which you did not live. I say that I imagine this hypothetical word would be German, with no direct English equivalent. I long to let her soak in the warm pool of memories that flood my temporal lobe and light up my hippocampus. That time was my queer coming of age comparable perhaps to high school or college days for more well-adjusted, normative folks. I fell in with an amorphous band of creative misfit geniuses and sexual outlaws and it was there that I first discovered my own personhood, a self and somebody who could explore and fuck up and expand and make art and fuck and still be someone worthy of love. I smile and paste the layers of time together, imagine B delirious and sweaty on the dancefloor at Muff Dive, making out with other dykes in the dank graffiti-brindled men's room where the girls back their asses up to the urinal to piss. Weren't there always trans women back then, in our messy packs, bellied up to the bar, hooking elbows with us in the pit at shows as we skanked in the chaos like links of a chain, gender was a wet paper bag we all were busy punching our way out of so we could choose what we jumped back in to. In this *MAD* fold-in of my chronology, the past and present press in toward each other to make a seamless picture. But on some days the misty glowing corona of memory fades and in the harsh light of last call I can't see the me of now, nor the B of now, neither of us, in that picture.

I find one German word, it's close, but not quite right: *Sehnsucht* (*[ˈzeːnzʊxt] or zeen-zhot*) – a German noun that denotes an intense longing or pining, a deep emotional state; sometime it is used to describe life's longings. Perhaps it encompasses something of our unfinished business, the repairs we never managed to make, the canvases leaning unfinished against a cinderblock wall.

My friend B is a lesbian trans woman. She is ten years younger than me, and even younger in trans years. I love hanging out with her because she's smart and funny and alive; she's a smokejumper who can parachute into the fire of any social situation and she will meet it with the sheer power of her extroversion. She's game for just about anything. Despite the shitty stuff she's experienced in life, her compass always swivels to a magnetic north of positivity, and in that way we are alike. We both relish the feast of tonight like survivors, like we might be dead tomorrow. Because we both know that we might be. We both know that life is fleeting and ephemeral and filled with impossible brutality and loss and also the most gorgeous messy joys and phosphorescent blazes of connection and why not gather as many of those fragile branches of light to your breast as you can and try to build a nest? Why not magnify those tiny glowing pinpoints of sex and love and art and other fleeting parallels and draw a line between them all, why not make them a constellation that you can point your ship toward on the darkest nights? How ever can we make it so that you can see the body of all your myths in the sky?

"To look forward to the history that will be, one must look at and retell the history that has been told" ~ Jonathan Goldberg, *The History That Will Be*

B has a stamina and enthusiasm for dating that is entertaining to listen to and leaves me a little breathless. *Is this what I sounded like in the zenith of my dating prowess*, I wonder. B often wants to talk about her lesbian identity, like, she is really fucking excited about it. I don't think I've ever had such long conversations about being a dyke, even when that's what I was perceived to be, even when that was the default identity that felt better than anything else I could possibly conceive of for myself. *Butch* was an apartment I could fit most of myself into and live happy there a little while. But B is so happy to be a lesbian. I think if politics around Michfest hadn't been so fucked up, she would have been over the moon there. That shit was *made* for a woman like B. She belongs.

A while back another trans woman in my town was angry at me for performing with a group that I've been involved with in some way for over twenty years. She said she was tired of how all the trans men get a free pass. *Free*, I want to say, *do you know how many women I had to get off to get here*? But in all seriousness, I do understand her pain. And she is right: she, too, wants to be embraced in a community of queer women, accepted as a co-conspirator; and from where she's standing, it appears that I have the access I've always had to the sense of community of my butch past, which isn't accurate, but I can understand how it comes off that way to her, because it still is more connection than she feels like she has. I hate the sense of scarcity that pervades our trans community, the way we are always holding our sharpest knives up toward each other. In her eyes, I am privileged in my dyke history; in my skin I, too, long for that sense of community, of belonging. I wish she could see the extent of my lonesome, the way I can walk right up to queer women I know in public only to have them look away, until I say hello. As a bearded, precariously near middle-age man, I am to be avoided. I am unseen. I miss that feeling of striding into a space to be greeted by the folks in my community. She and I are both outsiders twirling alone in the soggy sawdust of an empty dancefloor. I am sad that we trans folks are often so deep within the cocoons of our own pain that we cannot make refuge for each other.

B reads *Valencia*, which describes circles of people I was running with at that time, and she tells me she is jealous. I tell her stories of my early twenties in dyke-run San Francisco. We didn't really run the city so much as we created self-sufficient microcosms within which we could thrive and create. We didn't own anything, we weren't the boss. But the worlds we fabricated by our raw knuckles and greedy mouths stretched a biosphere across the city and it was easy to imagine this entire place belonged to us, a feeling most of us had never had before or have had since. We roosted the city, claimed it, we were a noisy murder of crows laughing in the streets, fucking in the alleys, dancing and rocking out in bars, mounting shows in underground performance spaces, hosting orgies and play parties and confessionals in our bedrooms, planting our pirate flag along the bows of playground structures of our city. Every corner held our secrets. Sex was part of our art and we did a lot of both. We came together, our own Left Bank, and we appointed our own Gertrudes and Ernests and Pablos and Alices.

I discover another word: *Saudade* ([saw'dadʒi] or Soh-dah-zgche) – a Portuguese term that also has no direct corollary in English. It evokes a deep emotional state of nostalgic or profound melancholic longing for an absent object of one's love. The sense that the longed-for may be long gone is tamped down like a cigarette butt in the ashy bottom of one's heart. We pave over that ache with denial of the inevitable. The less one is sure of the missing target's whereabouts, this yearned for someone or something, the stronger this feeling will be. This isn't quite the right word B was looking for either, but it is getting warmer. *Saudade* might describe the pangs of hope of the widow in her watch, always scanning the crease between sky and sea for a ship some part of her knows will never return. *Saudade* perhaps describes the negative space, the hollow in your sheets which once housed your lover's warmth. While remembering an estranged lover with whom you never got to reconcile, *saudade* might speak to the pang of desire that survives in the desert of a dozen empty years between she and you. *Saudade* might be your reluctance to let go of that long lost love because in doing so you will have to finally relinquish childish love and learn to how to love like a grown man. But it is even more complicated, for *saudade* also means we find some pleasure, perhaps even joy within our wistful ache.

I'm gifted two tickets to an L7 reunion show, and of course I can't think of a better sidekick to take than B. I joke about how it is like a retirement party for old punk queers and I have a fucking blast despite my aching back and exhausted mind. I want to include B in a world of badass women which no longer includes me. I tell her about the time long ago I fisted a coworker for an art film, talked into it for the anonymity that later was blown on the big screen by my easily recognizable elbow tattoos. I tell her about the dyke-owned cafe I worked at as a short-order cook, of weekend brunch-rushes where we'd have the countertop seated shoulder-to-shoulder with hot queer women who ogled us as we sizzled up their food and plopped it onto thick porcelain diner plates, and how we loved every minute of our objectification under their hungry eyes.

My inclusion here was always conditional, so long as I played a part, stayed an erotic placeholder, kept my mouth shut. I kicked myself out before anyone else had a chance to exclude me. I might have stayed and subjected myself to the vulnerable ordeal of allowing myself to be known, to allow others to witness my growth. I robbed myself of that. Taking off was a survival skill I learned early on. There is much I lost in my itinerancy, my long wandering alone in the desert while I transitioned. There's something to be said for staying put and tending to your roots.

"The concept [of *saudade*] has many definitions, including a melancholy nostalgia
for something that perhaps has not even happened.
It often carries an assurance that this thing you feel nostalgic for will never happen again."
~ Jasmine Garsd, NPR

I can laugh at myself and my melancholic lament. I am such a different person, as anyone would be, close to two decades after my twenties and I would never want to go back. I am committed to the adventure of living, and finding out what comes next, even on my dark days. I do not regret transitioning, nor the choices I've made, even those I made when I didn't realize I had a choice. But I do miss that sense of easy belonging, the vibrancy and generosity of community, the playfulness and the trickster resiliency of that time and place. The swagger and the spit and the ferocity. The way we all found ourselves tossed together there, in this one time and place. I want B to feel that sense of belonging, a queer woman among other queer women, some of who might not be women, some of whom are not women yet, some of whom were always guys who felt at home with us, some who might leave queer identity behind like a thrifted sequin gown on a lover's chipped-paint hardwood floor.

"Some things you lose, some things you give away."
~ Sleater-Kinney, *Good Things*

I tell B about my time in this world, because she wants to know. I can be her eyes on the ground of the past. I want to share with B the class notes of a course I aced, even though it was never going to be my major. I want to share with her the films I watched in the early dawning of my awareness of my desire for women, the films that didn't quite reflect my interstices of my own desires and embodiment, but were an imperfect something; sometimes a great story that reflect your inside jokes back to you, put a soundtrack to your desires deemed forbidden by the world outside of your dome, other times something like a wave that you return until you realize it was for the person standing behind you: not intended for you but a friendly gesture nevertheless. I propose a late 80s-early 90s formative lesbian film fest. I want to show her "The Hunger", "Reform School Girls," "Go Fish," and "Bound." I imagine us laughing our asses off to Jennifer Tilly's amazing line: "Want to touch my tattoo, Corky?" The butch/femme depiction of "Bound" made us giggle uncomfortably in the red velvet seats of the Castro Theater, but despite the plucked eyebrows on the butch, it was closer to us than we could have imagined seeing on screen at that time. We imagined ourselves the noble outlaws, the ones who could get away with the money and the girl.

I want to teach my friend about a past that I loved but wasn't fully mine, a gorgeous vintage shirt that hangs in your closet full of stories but never fit you quite right. A moldering box of photographs carried from place to place. I want to teach my friend about a time that at least part of me felt at home and welcomed, a place where I could express some of my gender and be still loved in it. I want to bequeath this complicated playground to her, even though it is not mine to give and continues to turn to mulch beneath the more expensive heels of those who stomp those streets now, no longer in search of art or sex but of gelato and artisanal tacos and the grit and edge of our time burnishes into the pavement beneath the wheels of a monolithic tech company bus.

I want to tell my friend about the time I was living as a butch of sorts, how I was seen as a mannish woman and how there was joy to be found there for me even if it was a wave intended for the person standing near me, how even street violence and harassment and fists in my face and security guards pulling me out of restrooms only made me stronger in my resolve to not bow to anyone. I want to say how I was like Cool Hand Luke and I just kept getting back up. I want to make it sound like I was tougher than I really was. I want to confess that it is so much easier for me to own my own girlhood of sorts now that I am no longer bound by it, that I had get here to be able to be brave enough to see and love my own past selves. And sometimes I want to ask my friend about the boyhood she never inhabited but that I never got to have, if it felt like a friendly gesture intended for the person standing behind her, if there were things she loved and things she hated, if she is grateful for the pain because it shapes the woman she now can be. I want our children selves to go back in time and meet and plant a seed of being seen. I want our adult selves to whisper in each others' kid ears that in the future we won't be switching sides, there is no Point A to Point B, no train heading West and another heading East, no golden spike in the middle, we will whisper inaudible words while slowly tracing on each others' backs a spiral with our fingertips. There will be no adjoining gurneys where parts are swapped. We will each arrive someday as our own Pygmalion, carving our own forms the best we can from our own material and imaginations.

I want to hand over the keys to a kingdom I no longer have, left on my couch after a sweaty tussle, never really gifted to me, the hesitant occupancy of a dog that is suspected of having the capacity to bite and therefore betray. How can I give her something that was only condition-ally mine, but that I love like it was my own? I find myself in the role of unlikely link coupling her to a slice of lesbian life that is foreclosed to me. I daydream of starting a Big Sisters/Big Sisters program. Enlisting the dykes and lesbians and queer women I know to take a trans woman to lunch or a rock show, to invite her to join a writing group or art col-lective, to go thrifting or biking, to welcome trans women into their world of women, one relationship at a time. I imagine me, burly, bearded, middle-aged practically, brokering this peace deal among warring na-tions, and trying to convey the lives that would be saved when trans women become welcomed and protected by non-trans women. I imag-ine that noisy rookery in the high branched, the cackling of joy, the re-turn to that old punk dyke fuck you spirit that saved my life and can still save lives, for those who need it.

14

Mid-Life Transition

By Tygh Lawrence-Clark
Age 51, Transmasculine, Lesbian

[*Editor Note: Tygh has chosen to stay true to himself by maintaining his lesbian identity, an identity he embraced for over thirty years, and one he shares with his wife, also a lesbian. He spent fifty years waiting to feel comfortable with himself, and when he finally began living authentically and presenting as male, he has found the truth he had been seeking for all those years.*]

※※※

I remember never feeling right in my own skin. I remember hating my long hair, so I wouldn't take care of it and eventually it would become so knotted my mother would cut it, much to my delight. I remember hating dresses. All of my Halloween costumes were male characters. By the time I was in elementary school, I started having a recurring dream that persisted well into adulthood—I dreamt that I was a third gender, with both a penis and a vagina. It took me fifty years to figure out what this all meant.

It's not that I'm not thoughtful about life. I had a very abusive childhood, so I did not have the luxury of self-discovery when I was young. I was so worried about conforming to my mother's expectations in an attempt to avoid her form of discipline, that I did not have much energy for internal reflection. She did allow me to be a tomboy at times, but I could never voice to her my confusion or feelings about gender. I even dated boys just to please my mom and to fit in.

I came out as lesbian at seventeen, thinking this was the reason I was such a tomboy and attracted to women. My mother responded by having me committed to a psychiatric hospital (which I broke out of). So, I spent the next years of my life estranged from my family, and focused on survival. There were times when I was homeless and slept on the streets.

I eventually reconnected with my family and attempted to conform again by embracing my feminine attributes. This was not as hard as you might imagine, because I never wanted to be perceived as a butch lesbian. That never felt right to me. Life went on and I focused on work and relationships, never really finding my niche and never really sticking with anything, or anyone, for very long.

Fast forward twenty years and I find myself married to my soulmate, Sandi. After three years together, we decided to get married, as we lived in a state where that was possible at the time for same-sex couples. Sandi happens to be a psychologist who came out as lesbian later in life. As part of her work, she began participating in a training program for providing care to transgender clients, and would talk to me about things she was learning.

On New Year's Day 2015, we were taking a walk and Sandi said something about the transgender support group she was running. I suddenly stopped, looked at her, and said "I'm transgender." She looked at me and said "Ok." Two weeks later we attended *First Event* in Boston. For the first time in my life, I felt like I belonged. I finally knew who I was. Two months after that I had my first appointment at Fenway Health and started Testosterone. At the age of fifty, I was finally starting my journey to becoming my true self.

The hardest part, so far, was telling my eighty year old father who was raised in a very traditional culture. It ended up going well and he was supportive, telling me that he loves me no matter what. However, over time, things have become more difficult, as he continues to call me by my birth name, and in general has avoided direct contact with me.

Sandi has been amazing. Although she has struggled with maintaining her identity as a lesbian, we have been able to talk openly about this issue and have decided that we are both "hybrids." Although I love presenting as male, I do not want to lose my identity as a lesbian, and although she now presents as a straight female, she also wants to maintain her identity as a lesbian. This may sound strange to others, but it works for us. Unfortunately, we've come to realize that others do not support this perspective, as many friends have indicated that they do not understand why Sandi has stayed with me.

The easiest part of my transition has been my relationship our son Ben, who has always called me Mom. He actually was excited when I told him I am transgender, and he immediately switched pronouns and started calling me Popi. Since then, things have become more difficult because he is thirteen, so we are both going through puberty at the same time. Sandi hates this part of the whole thing!

The hardest part of transitioning has been the initial realization of the fact that I am trans. After living as a lesbian for thirty-three years, having this light bulb moment at the age of fifty has been quite daunting. I have lost a lot of friends...straight and lesbian... and some family members because of coming out. Another aspect of my personal struggle is being a transgender man of mixed race. I don't feel the "male privilege" that others talk about. I now sense that white women walk on the other side of the street and pull their children closer as I approach. Racist people are likely to challenge me as a dark-skinned man, more so than when I presented as a woman.

I also see that there is a level of competition amongst the trans community. Each person's journey is their own, their struggles are their own, and in no way should be compared to the next. We as humans should bond together. We all have to share this small planet, but there is so much prejudice against us out there that I think we at least should keep the trans bond and have peace within the community. We should all be real, and recognize when there is someone who is struggling just a bit more than we are. Put things into perspective and reach out your hand to those less fortunate. I'm hoping that talk and visibility of transgender people is not a fad. My hope is that the acceptance of trans people will follow a path that is similar to gay people. We, as trans people, have to stay visible and put ourselves out there.

Now that I have been on T for nine months, I am loving all of the changes. I have facial hair and my voice has deepened. I finally feel right in my body. This has especially been true since I had top surgery. I have always hated those things! It used to be that I refused to go clothes shopping and Sandi would try to go for me, but even then, after trying things on at home, I would be frustrated with how I looked. Now, with my flat chest and broad shoulders, I've become a shop-a-holic!

At the age of I'm fifty-one, I finally know who I am. It's never too late to transition, and live the life you are meant to live. I know I will continue to struggle with all of the issues mentioned above, but I have

A Herstory of Transmasculine Identities

no second thoughts. I'm finally me!

15

No Matter What You Do, You'll Always know

By Hunter T.
Age 59, Transman

[Editor Note: Some people just know when they are young, without a doubt, they are not a girl. In today's society, young people are being exposed to the term transgender younger and younger due to the media and Internet, as well as from the negative visibility in politics and religious circles, and they have the opportunity to voice their discomfort and their needs. Those who were born before the Internet, however, before anyone was aware of the prevalence of transgender people, there was, as Hunter says, "no language" to explain the feelings. In the mid-to-later 1900s, if a girl was attracted to other girls, it was likely she grew up and became a part of the lesbian community, whether or not she identified as a lesbian or not. Second-wave Feminism was widespread in the Sixties and Seventies, with the Third wave appearing in the early Nineties. Many lesbians became a part of these movements. If one was transgender, being a butch lesbian was the closest thing they knew to being able to live as a masculine individual and still have a community around them. Hunter shares what life is like, living with his true self being locked away for far too long, even once he had the "language," until someone close told him eight words he would never forget.]

❈❈❈

At an early age, I knew there was something different about me. I wasn't like other girls. In kindergarten, I had a girlfriend who lived a few houses down the street from me. I remember watching how the boys in my class interacted with the girls. That's how I learned. I even kissed my girlfriend a couple times.

When I was about eight years old, my family relocated from the Midwest to California, and this was a major culture shock. Within that same year of the move, I informed my parents that I wanted to be a boy. The expression on my mother's face told me everything I needed to know-there was no way I could tell her the truth. So I lied. I said that I wanted to be a boy so I could wear pants to school. This was prior to 1970, before girls and women could be allowed to wear pants to school or work. There was a look of relief on my mom's face. But I knew that my life had changed at that moment.

I knew that I could never tell anyone how I felt, I didn't think they would understand. I didn't have the vocabulary to provide a clear-cut answer, all I knew was that I wanted to be a boy. My younger sisters always referred to me as their 'brother,' but there was no real gender reference, just a figurative reference.

In the early 1970s, I was in high school, and it was during this time I realized I really liked girls. I even had a crush on a girl who lived up the street from our family. In fact, she and I are still friends today. I had even told her I loved her, like a brother.

After I graduated high school, I had a serious relationship with a girl. While she and I were dating, she met a guy and they began to date. That should've told me something about who I was. I enlisted in the U.S. Navy in 1976, and after boot camp at my first duty station, I found many other women who liked women in the same way I did, and we all played on the military base women's softball team. I got involved with a woman, and we soon moved in together. She and I shared some commonalities; both of us were on the same end of the male spectrum. Around that time, the term "lesbian" became popular and became the go-to way to identify women who liked or loved other women.

I never did like that term, *Lesbian*. Of course, identifying as a lesbian had its rewards; I was in a woman's body, and I loved other women, so I must've been a lesbian. Yet, I always felt strange, as though I was *pretending* to be a woman. There were times when I thought I was 'found out' because I would do or say something so out of the ordinary for a woman…but not so out for a man.

Throughout my life, I was aware of various people who had transitioned male-to-female; first was 'Christine Jorgensen'; then years later, there was the tennis player, Renee Richards. My mom had even showed me an article that was written in the mid-1970s in a *Cosmopolitan* magazine about sex change surgery…but we never discussed the article.

It wasn't until the early 1980s when I heard about female-to-male transition, and I was amazed at how many women who decided to transition. I was shocked that they dared to try, and disappointed in myself that I didn't have the guts. At that time in my life, however, there were too many fears, concerns, and major obstacles placed in my way to consider female-to-male transition.

About fifteen years later, another wave of butch-identified lesbians chose to transition from female to male. My heart ached for an opportunity, but I remembered the look on my mother's face when I told her I wanted to be a boy; I knew if I had decided to transition, that it would break her heart.

For the past fifty years, I've hidden that part of me. All of my desires to be male were locked away in a vault. And, just like a time capsule, that vault has opened. At first, the sense of freedom was very evident. It wasn't until almost one year later, that my feelings, my dysphoria, began to appear. These feelings emerged from the vault – and with it came the anger. I then understood why I would always have a chip on my shoulder attitude. For fifty years, I'd been angry.

I had been angry because I'd lived a lie. I was raised in a time where my feelings didn't matter, where I had to learn to hide my feelings, and where I had to learn how to 'fit in'. Except that it didn't matter where I turned, I was never able to find that place of serenity where I felt I belonged. I never got the feeling that I belonged when I 'came out' nor when I got sober, two of the biggest life-changing events. I didn't get that feeling of belonging until my cousin uttered the phrase – "*no matter what you do, you'll always know.*"

That phrase unlocked the vault. The same vault I kept my darkest secrets about my true identity, and within three weeks of that conversation with my cousin, I knew that I would transition female to male.

All my life, I've always felt different—like I didn't fit in anywhere. In my mind's eye and what I saw in the mirror's reflection as I walked by— they were not the same thing. And I would get angry. I did not understand why the images were different. For that reason, I don't to this day like seeing pictures of myself, because what they look like in print is not the same image I see.

I felt that even as a butch lesbian, I never fit in there, either. It wasn't that I wasn't butch enough; God knows I was a card-carrying, butch leatherdyke. The point was that I felt I was living a lie. Somehow, I knew I was different. Different in a way that even though I lived as a woman, I felt that I was pretending. So my actions, the way I dressed, the way I spoke, the way I walked, and even the way I ate, I had to pull back so I could fit in with other women. But I always felt like I was a guy pretending to be a woman, even though outside, I presented as a woman—butch as that may have been—the bottom line was that my body still presented me as a woman. That was *my* dysphoria.

I've had a few long-term relationships, the longest of which lasted almost thirteen years. Ironically, we broke up because she wanted to date men, and the guy she married looks a lot like me. Other relationships I had lasted about four to five years, but there was always something missing in the connection between her and me. As I look back, I realize that while the outside of me looked female, as the relationship progressed the truth was women want that female connection. I really didn't have enough of the female connection they wanted, and that's what eventually ended some of my relationships.

Shortly after my conversation with my cousin, who also transitioned, MTF, I made the decision to transition in October 2014. Once I declared that, I started to use male pronouns and identified as male, and I stopped attending female only or female-identified events, activities, etc. I understood the value of having women-only spaces. The women in my life support my decision to transition.

I've been very fortunate to live in Seattle, where transitioning is simply a way of life. On May 22, 2015, I started HRT. Today, it's been nine months on testosterone; my life is good. I'm out to my family, to my work, and pass very easily as a man 98% of the time. The only obstacles have been my own insecurities and fears.

It has been fifty years since I first spoke up about wanting to be a boy. Now that little boy gets the opportunity to grow into a man.

16

My Invisible History Dilemma

By Stephen Ostrow
Age 25, Non-binary,
Transmasculine,
Nonmale, Queer

[Editor Note: Stephen's essay does not need an introduction. His unique, emphatic and somewhat poetic approach to examining identity, society's constructs and systems will speak for itself.]

❋❋❋

Let's talk about the human condition. One condition. Interwoven amongst all the other contributing conditions that summate to create the human condition. Let's talk about identity.

An identity. Gender identity.

Identity is a multi-layered, often convoluted subject for which enough time and effort is not allocated. Seldom does one come to understand their self, let alone anyone else. It is my experience that an overwhelming majority of people accept the identities they are assigned. In our "modern culture" of microwave-ready meals we also have prepackaged identities which we are assigned and to which we ascribe. Sometimes we ascribe to these packages begrudgingly and bleed out of the cellophane, and sometimes we agree that this form holds our figure well. Based on the package we are ascribed or ascribe to, thusly we are labelled throughout life. So what happens when we bleed out of the package? When we repackage ourselves? When we have cognitive dissonance about the subsequent subscription of labels assigned? I'll tell you what I do, I dismantle and disassemble the labels. Thing is, there are not precise instruments for this process. Human conditions do not exist in a vacuum. Identity is part internal and part external, part individual feelings of belonging juxtaposed with the perception and interpretation of others.

We are all coming out of our binary boxes of duality over and over again. We must support each other through that process.

Here is a glimpse at my invisible history dilemma.

The day before the flight to carry me back home, my sister, whom I will never have the honor to know, was murdered. Brutally slain. Stripped away from this world, on the grounds of my alma mater.

Though I feel the tremendous weight settling in my chest, this body chokes back the tears burying the sorrow in fear and anger and rage.

Let us talk about Transmisogny.

Let us demand Feminism.

When I think that the only "protection" I have is other's perception of my masculinity and whiteness...Which are fundamentally flawed social constructs built on lies, stacked on a classist hierarchical capitalist power play in which hard cocks are the primary construction tool...

Isolation, fear of violence, if I feel it so strongly from my privileged place, the insurmountable Suffering that must exist for my siblings on the feminine spectrum is utterly unacceptable by any moral variation of humanity. So what I hear is that my mere existence is so problematic...

Wait, let's back up a moment so that this piece of my puzzle finds cohesion in the mind, and I'm hopeful—the heart.

So, I'd like to share with you that I look like a "man" and have a vagina. Now, lots of people that also have vaginas are aware that their vagina is not the only directly correlated complex combination of stuffs that embodies their self-expression. In my experience, people with penises find this concept harder to grasp—pun intended. But let's think together for a moment that this experience of mine is a by-product of our culture rather than genitals; a by-product of our constructs rather than hormones; a by-product of society rather than chromosomes. Scientifically our genitals are composed homologous tissue. Yes, each of us has a pussy and a dick, a clit, a cocklit, dicklit, gummy bear, juicy organ and some round things whether they dangle or nestle and none of it has all that much to do with how you feel inside. Each of us carries a complex array of combinations of hormones and chromosomes that are impacted through fetal development and every single micro-moment of our lives by our internal and external environment.

Being sorry and Trans in this world is too redundant. As Mother Marsha would say—"Pay it no mind, Honey."

So, the other day I answered the phone at the domestic violence hotline where I work midnight shift. My 5-o'clock shadow in tow and...

That day a woman called me ma'am.

Never before have I ever been more comforted by the use of a pronoun in reference to me. It is the opposite of what one may think. It doesn't make sense, not completely—even to me; however, it is my experience—it is me, it is circumstantial and holds so much meaning. You see, I spent twenty years uncomfortable with "she" and then I spent six endowed with "he." I have come to learn it is not the word that I have striven for but the tone and intention behind it, the genuine respect and unconditional human regard that has been lost in the binary. The binary, a construction zone where everything is sexualized and monogamized and hetero/homo normalized and -ismed and boxed and bowed and made pretty to disguise that underneath we are all raw and exposed to the elements that condition humans. But it's unacceptable to accept, acknowledge and express vulnerability, especially publicly.

When I was called she, I was thusly assumed to be meager and weak, unable to lift air and wrong to think, incapable of speaking intelligibly and contributing to society... Society which is made by and for him. When I was called he, I was deemed to be better than, more than, stronger than, the most capable and responsible for the perpetuation of the systems in place that are fundamentally flawed and oppressive and demeaning.

Having been informed by second wave feminism that my body is my own, and later re-informed by third wave that the rules only apply within the narrow confines of birkenstocks or hysterectomy (in which the binary form of femininity is retained), I was dysphoric with my body so I took steps to change it when I was called she. It was not about the word, but about inner peace. It was about being able to find solace in the temple of my body, which ultimately terminated my binary-formed femininity. When I was called he, I was dysphoric about society and its perception of me. I was constantly associated by socially constructed identification to be of a group that I have never fathomed I could ever be;

White Male.

When a construct is our only exposure, when it is all that we see, it is all we perceive, and it is all we think we can be-but there is so much more and there is fluidity that cannot be seen in the hard lines of these coded confines because our relative reality is grey.

I am not attempting to bribe you into concession or even sway you into unexamined agreeance. My experience is fraught with disjointed personal opinions and contrary happenings that combine to create a shitton of cognitive dissonance. This is not my attempt to find resolve. This is a description of the condition manifest by patriarchy that has entrapped and enslaved us all. From our beliefs about the conditionality of human worth, to the actions carried out by rape culture informed by poverty mentality (which, by the way, is a subsect of patriarchy) that is destroying the planet which we inhabit.

From my lens, through this periscope, when one looks, one gains momentary clarity about the devastating intersectionality of racism, sexism, classism, first world Narcissism, the praise of our conformity, and learned lack of positive regard...Each of us embody the propensity to perpetuate these oppressive systems, and equally the power to destroy the status quo and create a space where on an individual level we can all examine and discern our own true identities.

Identities that open boxes, identities that progress along a nonlinear spectrum of human expression. Because, with faith I do believe just as science and faith must complement one another for a semblance of validity, our personal identities must complimentarily inform and peacefully relate to our underlying vulnerability.

17

My Experiences Have Shaped Me

By Lucas Aiden Wehle
Age 23, Transman

[*Editor Note: Like others, Lucas, as a child, knew he was not a female. Again, the problem so many encounter is the lack of language in voicing this knowledge. We go through life resisting the boxes we are put into while knowing we do not fit into these prescribed boxes. Some discover the lesbian community and attempt to make it their home, but it isn't long before the truth is realized that they still aren't in a place of inner peace. Lucas explains why, even after his transition, he continues to embrace his feminist past, and how discrimination has played a part in his life then and now, and how he has learned to overcome.*]

****

The irony about growing up is that we're told we can be whatever we want to be by the same people who have placed you in a box from the moment you were born. Before we even take our first breath on earth, society has planned our entire lives for us based on one small thing: our genitalia.

I cannot recall a time when I wasn't sure I was a man. What I didn't know was how to explain this knowledge to the people around me. For a long time I didn't even know the word trans or that anyone else identified the way that I did. I thought I was the only person who felt this way and that my life would be miserable.

My childhood was filled with masculine toys; I wore masculine clothes; and donned the most masculine haircut I was allowed, for the majority of my life. I remember when my parents would get defensive when strangers called me "he", but I didn't mind at all! Once puberty hit, I was forced to wear more girl clothes. That was when gender dysphoria got real for me.

I would get in screaming arguments with my parents and sister about what I was going to wear to social functions- but unfortunately I rarely won. For a brief time in high school, I tried to force myself into the box that the world told me I belonged in, only to find myself buried in a hole overwhelmed with depression. No matter what I did, I could not seem to find happiness anywhere I searched. So instead, I tried to make everyone around me happy by continuing to pretend to be something I was not.

My confidence suffered and as a fix I searched for love. I found myself trapped in an abusive relationship with someone who told me that I would never be able to find love elsewhere. It was an unhealthy situation and it took me almost a year to find my way out of it safely. This only worsened my mental state and pushed me further away from telling anyone how I really felt inside.

Even after I discovered the trans community and became educated on what it meant to be trans, I struggled to come out because I feared that no one would accept me or love me anymore. It wasn't until college that I found an LGBTQ organization who gave me the love and support I needed to feel comfortable enough to be true to myself.

With the help of my friends and (at that time) girlfriend, I finally found the strength tell someone I was trans for the first time. I will never forget how it felt the first time someone addressed me as "he" or called me handsome. It gave me hope because for the first time in my life, I didn't have to hide. Without the support from my friends and resources from my community, I wouldn't have made it to where I am today.

Coming out to my family was the hardest aspect of my transition. When I first told them I was trans, the shit hit the fan (and although I thought I was prepared for the worst) they still don't respect my identity today. They really fought against it for a long time, arguing it was a phase and telling me I will always be a girl. I guess they are still fighting considering after 5 years they still refer to me as my birth name and use feminine pronouns- sometimes even in public.

During the first couple years of my college career, I was one of the only trans people on campus who was out and open to sharing my identity with others. During this time, I realized how important it was to educate others about the trans community; it was a topic that is so rarely discussed. Being as involved as I was in the LGBTQ community, I had a lot of friends who identified as lesbians prior to and during the last 5 years of my transition that are also now "out" as trans men. I am thankful for all the work that our TSU put in to make our university a safer environment for students to feel comfortable coming out as trans.

Before I came out as trans, I did identify as a lesbian for a few years of my life. However, I never felt comfortable with that identity because I did not see myself as a woman. Today, I identify as a straight, trans man and by straight I do not mean I only date women with vaginas. My sexuality does not discriminate based on anatomy. Rather, I am attracted to femininity or feminine-identifying people. In fact, I prefer trans women because I feel that the connection I share with them is stronger than a bond I could have with someone who does not understand my experiences through transition.

I have always assumed a masculine role in my relationships. I think that some of my attraction to femininity is because I prefer to be the masculine person in relationships. I am not saying that relationships have to have traditional "masculine" and "feminine" roles, I am simply saying that is how my personal relationships usually play out.

My current partner is a trans woman and as I mentioned before, the connection I have with her is golden. Our relationship is special because we have the same (but opposite) experiences and we both identify very strongly with our queer bodies. Our identities and our experiences blend so beautifully together and I cannot imagine having a more intimate connection with anyone else.

Something I am very aware of is the male privilege I gained with being perceived as a cisgender man to most. I have always been a feminist and will always continue to be. However, the way my feminist identity is perceived by others has shifted quite dramatically since my gender transition. For example, people that don't know I'm trans might think it is atypical that I am a feminist since most men don't openly identify as such. I find that most men don't share my views about how women should be respected.

I am a feminist because I believe everyone should have equal rights regardless of gender identity, sexual orientation, race, ethnicity, class, or any other social construct we have created. I am a feminist because ALL WOMEN are women and deserve to be treated with as much respect as every cisgender man in this world. I am a feminist because all genders, not just those that fall on the binary, should be acknowledged and respected. Finally, I am a feminist because (regardless of my trans identity) I believe that as a man I have to recognize my privilege and use it as an advantage to demand equality in all aspects for all people.

Despite my privilege, I have experienced discrimination because of my gender identity. I used to be a very religious person and was extremely involved in church during my adolescent years. I was a youth leader, was in several praise bands, and rarely missed an event the church hosted. Yet, none of that mattered to them when I opened up about who I really was. After coming out, I was kicked out of my church and the people who were supposed to be my family turned their backs on me when I needed them the most.

In addition to religious discrimination, I am also among the large number of trans individuals who have experienced physical violence in response to my identity. During my junior year in college, I was attacked and threatened in a bathroom by a peer in my program that knew I was trans. He wanted to make it clear that my kind were not welcomed in the men's room.

All of my experiences have shaped me into the person I am. Although my journey has been unique and challenging, I would not change the way I was born or socialized even if I could because I know I wouldn't be the same. I know that my life has been full of experiences that will help me impact other people around me. My trans identity has made me stronger, wiser, more independent and more mature than I might have been otherwise. I am very proud of the man that I am today and I wouldn't change anything that got me here. I love my story, just the way it is. But most importantly, I (finally) love myself.

18

Waiting For the Third Line

By Day Walker
Age 50, Transmasculine/Agender

[*Editor Note: Sometimes there is just no terminology that can describe who we are in terms of gender identity; we learn all the words, but none are appropriate to embrace. We try some of them on, one by one, but none are "just right." Day has spent life looking for a place to fit in, but there is still something critically lacking in our society and Day has spent years trying to find the third choice in a world full of binary.*]

✕✕✕

I was born in 1965 and raised in the Oakland Bay Area, California. This is a short story of how I came to recognize who I truly am inside and out.

I was 5 years old when I recognized that I was attracted to the female of our species. I crushed heavily on my Kindergarten teacher. I was sent home from school once with a note pinned to my shirt for pulling up the girls' dresses on the playground. My poor Mom must have been horrified. By the age of 7, I recognized that events like this made me different. That never frightened me, in fact I'd say that I was a bit perplexed as to why it made me different. As an adult, in hindsight, I had already begun to separate gender from sexuality. By the age of 10 – I found myself looking for a third line to stand in. Teachers would tell us to line up, boys on one side and girls on the other and I stood there waiting for option #3 that would be for people like me. It never happened.

The day I can remember feeling the most awkward was the day my Mom told me I had to put a shirt on at the beach. I pointed at my boy siblings and protested *'How come they don't have to wear a shirt?'* I was made aware of, and felt ashamed of my developing body for the first time.

By the age of thirteen, I was convinced that the reason why human bodies only came with choice A and choice B was solely for the purpose of procreation. That the laws of attraction, AKA sexual preferences, were steered by our minds and souls and open to explore beyond that which conformed to the hetero-normative restrictions placed upon one's Gender. Of course, as a child I could not describe things as I know them now.

All hell broke loose in my head the day I found out there were several 'dirty words' for folks like me. Lesbian. Dyke. Gay. I digressed. I learned what these words meant and still could not relate to them. To me, I wasn't 'female' and I wasn't 'male'. The term Lesbian sounded like something one would need to take antibiotics for. It felt icky to be called Lesbian. I never embraced specific terms that equated to 'gay woman'. I did, however, embrace the umbrella term of 'Gay'.

I had always imagined myself to grow up to be just like the rock and roll folks I idolized. All the long haired hippies fascinated me. I never cut my hair short to conform to the idea of what 'Butch' looked like. Easy rider posters were found pinned to my walls, along with David Lee Roth and Robert Plant. But I never saw them as men, just people I related to and fancied that I would grow up to look just like them. (And I did).

Fast forward. My career happened to develop into over twenty-five years in the Motorcycle Industry in the Oakland Bay Area. I was often recognized for being the 'first woman' to do things in a male dominated field. The first 'woman' to manage a multiple brand Dealership in California. The first 'woman' Service Manager at a well-known Harley Davidson Dealership was the one that seemed to break through the gender barriers within that Industry. I fought hard to be recognized for my skills in the field, not to be recognized as the first 'woman' to conquer certain aspects of the industry. I had to deal with misogyny on a daily basis. And male privilege. I called it out when it seemed necessary, but still felt strange doing so, as I still did not see myself as either gender and wondered if I was speaking out of turn because of this. Which leads me to...

The internet. This is where I learned more about myself than any book could ever teach me. I was introduced to the Butch/Femme Community online. This was also my first glance at Transgender folks. I basked in the diversity within the BF Culture. All-inclusive never looked so beautiful to me. It was there that I found a term that was closer to describing me than any other had thus far. Gender Neutral. I was Butch, Gender Neutral and I had found my chosen family. I became a veteran of the Forums, participating in many difficult conversations spanning from how we 'queers' moved about in the 'straight world' to why we seem to still judge one another even within our own Community. Now I host five Facebook Groups for those who feel at home within the BF Community, and make it a personal goal to share knowledge I have gathered with the newer generations. Inter-generational connections are more important than at first it may appear. And now...

At the age of fifty, I have found myself all over again. I wasn't Gender Neutral at all. I was/am Agender – also known to some as Trans-masculine. I had, up to this time in my life, always pretty much ignored my biologically female born body and moved about the world at large by piloting things from just my mind and soul. It wasn't that simple anymore. I began a long trek with depression and dysphoria. I chocked it up to being symptomatic to my diagnosis of Multiple Sclerosis. I could not have been more wrong. With the support of my wife of twelve years now, I began to look into my options for HRT. It was like the sand finally disappeared from beneath my feet that day. The day I truly found peace with who I am inside and out. I do not identify as Transgender. There would be no surgeries, and no changing of the gender marker on my ID. I would, however, be growing myself a long beard and mustache and finally evolve into the imagery of those I had always idolized as a child. This is confusing for some people to understand, but I am not evolving for them. *I am evolving for me.*

Here's where I am today: I am 4 months into hormone replacement therapy and could not be happier. However, I now find myself struggling a bit with 'space.' I'm still taking up space in the BF Community, but have also involved myself in the Transgender online Community where I feel as though my journey differs vastly from many others and I wonder if I am taking up space that belongs to those who solely identify as Transgender. It seems to mimic the feelings that I experienced as a child. I'm still looking for the third option to appear. The box marked 'Other'. I still feel like I do not belong in the 'girls' line or the 'boys' line. The difference now is that I know there are more folks just like me out there in the world and am grateful for the opportunity to share with you all -

A Herstory of Transmasculine Identities

my story of being 'other gender'.

19

The Unexpected Costs of Living Authentically

By Jackson Jantzen
Age 44, Trans/Transman/
FTM/transmasculine

[*Editor Note: Being a part of the more visible part of the LGBT community, those who are lesbian and gay, can give one a sense of belonging, a place that feels like a home, and people to call family; it is an experience and a connection shared. Upon transition, however, it is common for transmasculine people to suddenly appear on the "outside" of the community; though they still "feel" like part of it, the special, unique connection is oftentimes severed when a person transitions. Jackson shares his experiences being a male in society, and how his patterns of communication and behaviors have been forced to change due to societal perceptions.*]

❈❈❈

No two stories about the journey of discovering an individual's relationship to the world can be the same. We see differences based on our family make up, religious influences, geographic cultural makeup, and a thousand other things that form and shape our experience of the world. These become an important part of the conversation because the embodiment of these experiences frame what we fear, love, hate or value at the deepest level of our core. That journey makes us who we are in the world, how we love, and ultimately shapes those things we grow to value.

The journey is designed to provide us every conceivable feeling. You can't really know what joy, belonging or support is, until you know what it is to experience those elements you need lifting up from, whether it be pain, isolation, fear or the many other factors that all of us have faced.

Transitioning was the most critical, important thing I've done in my life to save my life. It has changed how I experience the world and who I am in the world in the best ways possible. We often talk about all of the good things that come from finally discovering the level of authenticity that is right for us, but it didn't come without a cost. It is my belief those reflections are just as important. I never imagined the defining moment of what would create such joy, sense of placement in the world and a long awaited comfort in my own skin would be a paradox of loss. Let me provide some context.

I was five years old and my mom was letting me walk the 1 block distance to kindergarten for the first time by myself. *"Are you a boy or a girl?"* I heard from a distant voice across the street, followed by the glares of three kids about three to four years older than myself. It's a moment that stuck in my memory, not only because it was the first time of many I would hear that question or learn that I was different, but it marked the day my innocence died. It was the last day that I would leave the house unaware of how my gender expression would impact my experience of the world.

I grew up in Texas in the late 70s and 80s. It's a cultural environment that rewards gender conformity. If you are female, you had better be striving to be the head cheerleader, not the quarterback. Pompoms just weren't for me and I embraced the label "Tomboy". I had no language for how I felt about my gender. In those days the hints and pleas I made to my parents related to gender did not have the current framework or language and they didn't know how to read it or help me. Ultimately, I knew my relationship to my gender was one I couldn't change and also knew that it made my navigation of the community I lived in more challenging. I spent so much energy trying to fly under the radar and just survive high school, I didn't dare to mentally or intellectually explore my relationship to sexual orientation and had no clue exploring my relationship to gender was an option.

The day after my high school graduation I moved to California. It was pivotal for me, providing me a freedom to explore my relationship to the world.

I quickly came out as a lesbian, and for the first time felt like I was part of a community. It wasn't the first time I'd encountered the lesbian and gay community. My father came out to me when I was eleven, but I had secretly known he was gay since I was about eight. It was right around the time the AIDS crisis hit and I watched silently and intently, not knowing yet how the disease was transmitted, but terrified at the prospect of potentially losing my father. I watched our government's lack of response to the crisis and also laid witness to my own church shun our organist who was fading before our eyes as he lost his battle with the disease. As I sat, feeling helpless and watching this piece of our history unfold, I also watched a group of friends and strangers made up of lesbians and gay men come together and create family for those disowned and dying.

Leading up to that time, I spent just about every Sunday morning in Sunday school learning through stories what an amazing and compassionate man Jesus was documented as being. It was hard not to want to emulate that. It was a pivotal moment for me as I watched not only those in my congregation, but those religious leaders with a voice across the national landscape who called themselves Christians behave in every possible way that contradict the behavior they said I was to emulate through the stories taught.

In the same moments, I watched this community of gay men and lesbians come together as an embodiment of all of those Sunday school lessons. As a friend of my father fought this disease, I witnessed the support network they created for him and others in the community. Strangers stepped forward to become friends and surrogate family for those disowned and discarded when they became ill. I watched them deliver meals and comfort, filling a void that families, churches or government proved unwilling to provide. They stepped forward, sometimes at personal risk to job, family or security to fight for resources and a larger response to the crisis, ultimately creating awareness and visibility.

I was raised Christian, but I learned more as to what it looked like to walk an honorable and righteous path from those gay men and lesbians than I ever did through the actions of the collective of faith communities in my prevue. It was one of the foundations that made me proud to be part of a community of people who had an incredibly strong ethic for caring, compassion and human equality.

I was eighteen when I finally was able to come to terms with my own orientation and came out as a lesbian. For the first time in my life, I felt a sense of belonging and when in lesbian or gay spaces, I felt safe, accepted, and like I'd found home. I loved the moment of connection when I caught the eye of a gay man or lesbian on the street and without a word and just a glance, have a moment of shared connection. It's a remarkable thing to share a silent moment with a total stranger and with one glance, know that intersections of your life and struggle are shared, honored and validated.

It wasn't until my thirties did my avoidance about my personal relationship to my gender identity really start to take a toll. Despite growing up in the age of Renee Richards, for many years I didn't have language nor understanding for how my experience of my body and gender was different from my sexual orientation. But as I gained more understanding, I still found a desire to run from it. The thought of losing the only community I ever felt a sense of welcoming or belonging created a huge sense of resistance for me. I had no clue how I'd fit into this community after transitioning. After many years and a growing depression that scared me into action, I finally sought help to learn what I needed to live more authentically.

Once I began transitioning I found relief in physical form, but had new struggles now. I didn't know how I'd fit into this community I'd grown to adopt as a pseudo family. Transitioning made me feel once again like I was on the outside looking in. I no longer had those moments of silent, knowing glances with LGBTQ folks on the street. For the first time I didn't clearly wear parts of my identity in my embodiment that led me to be "out" before I even spoke. I missed that sense of connection through shared experience and I quickly learned seeking those silent moments of connections with other trans folks were not typically welcome. So many in our community take pride in "passing" or seek to live stealth and acknowledgment of identity often led many to view it as a momentary failure to their efforts. The moment I so treasured of knowing I was not alone in the world through an exchange of a smile or nod no longer was safe or appropriate. Ultimately, learning to acknowledge a stranger as a trans brother or sister could easily cause pain, discomfort, dysphoria or depression instead of kinship or community.

Transitioning taught me a lot through some unexpected learning moments. My six-foot linebacker frame made my transition feel rather seamless and learning to move in the world as a man became the next point of challenge. For the first time in my life, I really know what it felt like to stand taller, more confident and proud. After a lifetime spent unsuccessfully trying to be invisible in the world in a large gender non-conforming body, I started to experience invisibility in some positive ways. I moved freely without daily or even hourly glares, confrontations or someone asking me to justify or explain my existence. Those moments of accusations like, *"You're going into the wrong bathroom!"* or the questions such as *"Why don't you just wear a dress or a bit of make up or maybe let your hair grow?"* or *"Are you a boy or a girl?"*

Within a few months of transition, it all faded into the background. It was great, however it presented a new learning curve. I learned quickly that there were some levels of access or ease I had as a butch female I was unaware of until I began navigating the world in my new embodiment.

All of a sudden, my patterns of communication with straight men had to change. I could no longer be the teddy bear I'd grown into. Even with some of the men I'd known for quite some time, tensions strained if I forgot for a moment about my shift in appearance and leaned in for a hug. Editing how I had become comfortable emotionally engaging with the world was a sad adjustment I realized I had to make for purposes of safety.

The hardest lesson for me to experience was the violence I now wore solely due to my shift in embodiment as male in our society. It wasn't apparent to the world I was raised and socialized female. The filter people often used to read my softer edges were gone. It was first demonstrated when I was in an airport waiting for a connecting flight. It was a scene I had experienced many times before I had transitioned without issue, but this time it was different. An adorable 3-4 year-old and her dad were about eight feet from the seat I waited in. She was happy and playful and just creating joy for those around her. I noticed her and then smiled, looking to the father to let him know how cute and adorable she was. Before I could even form an expression or sentence to speak, my eyes caught his piercing glare at me. He read me as this adult male and potential predator and it broke my heart.

It was the first in many lessons that a history of violence that I haven't fed nor do I want to own, but now embody solely due to outward reflection of maleness. It's an unfortunate legacy I am even more acutely aware of, am learning to navigate and ultimately fight against when possible. It has been reinforced in moments since when I've accidentally startled a woman who wasn't expecting me to be standing in a spot she wanted to occupy. Again a scene that had played out many times before, but now not only was her response a startled one, but it was accompanied by a momentary fleeting level of fear or terror.

Despite never feeling an attachment to my female embodiment nor any regret for transitioning, I sit with moments of mourning the loss of freedom for the outward expression of compassion, empathy and love. Now that I nurture an authentic gender identity and expression, I find myself searching for ways to find balance in navigating with safety, our cultural expectations, yet allowing the same authentic levels of expression for my spiritual, emotional and intellectual experiences.

20

Straight Femme to Gay Man: A Feminist Transguy's Journey Home

By Avi Ben-Zeev
Age 51, Gay Transgender Man

[*Editor Note: As you learned in the earlier chapters, not all trans-masculine individuals come from the lesbian community, and not all are attracted to women. Some, like Avi, lived as a feminine heterosexual woman before beginning to live an authentic life of a gay transgender man. Avi takes us on his journey of his life pre-Avi and the experiences that taught him and led him to where he is today, a strong feminist gay transman who is dedicated to breaking down stereotypes together with a group of students and colleagues.*]

※※※

If I were to ask my pre-transition self how my experience in the world has differed from hers, she'd say: "how long do you have?" I close my eyes and imagine her, Talia, my previous incarnation in this same life. Her multicolored hair is long and curly. She's wearing a waist high faux fur black jacket over a 70s style semi-sheer metal gray sequin tank, short black leather skirt, Zebra patterned knee-high platform boots, a black leather cuff on her left wrist, and on the right, a bracelet made of doll eyes, with brown and blue irises and long lashes that open and close as she moves her hand to touch my shoulder.

"Look at you! It's like I've put on middle age lumberjack drag!" she exclaims.

"Honey, you look faux queen fabulous, and I do miss you sometimes, but I've never felt more comfortable in my skin," I smile.

As a psychology professor and researcher, I am acutely aware that a thought experiment about my pre vs. post transition similarities and differences is suspect. First, in a perfect experiment, she and I would 'split' physically and continue to lead parallel lives to control for important variables that are not directly gender related, like age, experience and so-called maturity. Second, there's this pesky psychological phenomenon called choice-supportive bias, which refers to people's retroactive tendency to attribute more positive qualities (both accurately and falsely) to an option they had chosen. Here goes, caveat emptor.

Talia was born and grew up in Herzlia, Israel, to a working class family. Her dad and grandpa were rumored to have danced in the streets when they found out that after two boys, Talia's mom had given birth to a baby girl. In the 3rd grade, Talia failed arithmetic, got kicked out of choir, and her parents were called into school for an urgent talk because she sat with her legs "too wide apart for a girl." She'd hear the phrase, "Sit lady like" from her dad numerous times throughout her childhood, yet she constantly defied lady-like behaviors. She wore boy clothes, played soccer, and got into fistfights, boasting bruises like badges of honor. Secretly, Talia liked Barbie dolls, which her parents took as a promising sign of normalcy, until she gave them all buzz cuts.

After school, instead of going home, Talia would visit with her grandma, Savta Rivka. Savta Rivka barely finished elementary school in Russia. When she came home one day after school, she witnessed her father being killed by the villagers because he was Jewish. This kind of lynching, called a pogrom, was common. A non-Jewish Russian man, whose life's mission became to save Jewish orphans, brought her along with a group of children to Palestine, which he thought of as the Promised Land for Jews, an alleged place of safety.

Savta Rivka did manual labor, there's a picture of her in my mind's eye using a hammer on a newly forged road, and eventually married the macho debonair, Simcha. Saba Simcha owned a construction company, dug wells, build the humble duplex we lived in and even fixed his own false teeth. Saba Simcha also served as the unofficial arbiter of our town. People came to him to solve disputes and his ruling was 'law.' Savta Rivka lived in this formidable man's shadow for many years until he died in his 80s. She insisted that Talia get an education so that Talia could have choices in life. She wanted her granddaughter to have what she never could, a life that did not depend on the brutality and kindnesses of male oppressors and saviors. It was in her grandma's kitchen that Talia learned her first lessons on feminism.

To the ritualistic safety of Savta Rivka's chores, Talia would some-times mindlessly drift into crooning in English.

"Oh, it's you! I thought it was the radio," Savta Rivka said. "I wish I could understand the lyrics."

Talia offered to teach her English, which Savta Rivka accepted with a youthful chuckle. Once a week Savta Rivka would give up her hard-earned afternoon rest while Talia donned a pair of frames, with no lenses, to appear more tutor like. Voila, like a magic trick, the kitchen was transformed into a makeshift classroom. The orphaned Jewish girl turned grandma was a star student, her 8 year-old tutor cheering her on. The lessons began and ended with tea and chocolate cake made with low-grade cocoa powder, sugar, eggs, margarine, and flour, was moist on the inside with a blissful crusted brittle top. "Don't let a man dictate your life and please have sex before you get married," Savta Rivka advised with flushed cheeks, between sips of boiling tea and bites of the best chocolate cake in the world. In this magical kitchen, we had voices.

At the age of 12, to her complete bewilderment, Talia developed a woman's body. She wore shirts that were three times larger than her size and refused a bra. Men's gazes made her cringe and feel shame. When they touched her without consent, the word "no," mysteriously disap-peared from her lexicon. Finally, she decided to own this alien body. Transforming from tomboy into feminine drag, she found some power in oozing sexuality, wielding seduction as a weapon, which served her for a while but eventually backfired. In 2011, I published a paper on women's instrumental nonverbal flirtation under situations of intellec-tual threat. A reviewer commented: "Of course women use sexuality in a Machiavellian manner." "Fuck you!" I thought and revised the paper to be explicit about how social systems that are inherently sexist cause women to sometimes 'leak' flirtatious behavior, as a survivalist way of coping with powerlessness, and at a great risk to their well-being.

After finishing high school with failing grades and refusing to do mil-itary service, Talia fled Israel for Italy. She fell in love with Henry, a nice Jewish boy from NYC, who brought her to America. She married him to stay in the US legally despite loathing the institution of marriage. She warned him that she would never want kids.

Henry encouraged Talia to go to college. He went to Brown and she enrolled in Rhode Island College, across the tracks, the only college that would accept her given her dismal high school transcript, and conditional on whether she would pass elementary English and Math courses. Talia took notes in Hebrew while listening to lectures in English. She started caring about what her teachers thought of her, about doing well. Her heart would beat fast during exams and she'd be covered in cold sweat. Where did the shield of indifference go? She fell in love with psychology and started volunteering in a research lab. Talia's mentor praised her abilities but told her not to bother applying to an Ivy League school for a Ph.D. "Remember where you came from," he cautioned. With Henry's encouragement, she decided to do that anyway. In 1997, she received her Ph.D. from Yale, then went on to became a professor at Brown, Williams College and finally found an academic home at San Francisco State University. While at Brown, Talia left Henry, whom she still loved deeply. Narrative wise, it's tempting to attribute the divorce to her discovery of the category 'trans' – after all, before the internet, that possibility was as alien as becoming a Martian – but I'm doubtful that the explanation is that simple.

New Year's, 2016. I've been living in San Francisco for 15 years now. I look in the mirror and my 50-year-old reflection stares back at me wearing a different kind of gender drag: black boots, Diesel jeans that have an intentional worn out look, a t-shirt with a bear print, thick black hoodie with faux fur lining and a Ben Sherman military style gray and white striped cap. My facial hair is stylized – a thick goatee and sideburns, 70s style, hopefully giving more of an edgy than a creepy vibe.

I'm a gay transguy, which means that I am only attracted to men sexually and romantically. Early in transition the thought of having sex with cis gay men, especially the self-proclaimed gold star variety, terrified me. I voiced my fear to my trusted therapist, Adam, thankful for a safe space where I could be vulnerable.

"What if a gay guy gets so disgusted with my naked body that, you know, like in the movie the *Crying Game* he throws up?"

Adam paused then said decidedly, "Go forth, brave warrior, and have lots of sex with gay men. The *Crying Game* moment? I hope that happens sooner than later."

"What kind of therapy is this?" I asked.

"Aw, Avi," Adam grinned, "You won't die!"

"But I might just die a bit on the inside," I insisted.

"No you won't," Adam beamed, "I have complete trust in your resilience."

Encouraged if not completely convinced, I ventured boldly into the unknown, like a traveling salesman, knocking on doors with a suitcase full of silicon cocks in a variety of sizes, girths, colors and textures. My pitch: "Why settle for one when you can choose?" Sex run the gamut from boring to exciting, sometimes even meaningful and romantic, and I was just about to give up, gladly, on experiencing a vomit scene when I met a certain bear, a minister and a die-hard Giants fan, a good guy who read storybooks to dying children in his precious spare time.

"I have a question that's been nagging at me," he ventured. "What will happen if you take your clothes off and I..." he made a throwing up gesture and added some sound effects as if he were auditioning for a main role in a Hollywood remake of the *Crying Game*.

I laughed, a good hearty rolling laugh, "Thank you! My therapist would be pleased."

When I finally sit down to write the 'Cis Gay Man's Guidebook to Dating Transmen,' I'll make sure to include this advice, "Don't worry about offending us: We're a tough bunch and worst-comes-to-worst you'd only be embarrassing yourself."

I love being a gay man but sometimes I lament the narrowness of my desire, especially as a single guy looking to find a primary partner, in a large but shallow dating pool littered with fears-of-intimacy, stereotypes of maleness and masculinity, transphobia, and all too frequent deception. My sexual desire is definitely not about body parts. I love fucking men with self-proclaimed pussies and hairy boobs with hard-wired nipples. I hope that Mr. Right is out there somewhere, someone with a big... heart, to share life's moments in a cozy home with a white picket fence and a dungeon in the basement.

The feminist fire in my belly has grown, fueling me to become an ally, to leverage lived experience while reckoning with male privilege. My research centers on women's underrepresentation in science, technology, engineering, and mathematics (STEM) fields and is preoccupied with the homogenization of women and with misperceptions of female friendliness as signaling sexual intent by heterosexual men in academia and in the workplace. My Cognition and Social Equity lab explores how subtle situational cues, such as being in the physical minority in STEM environments, can cause women to experience a phenomenon known as stereotype threat, a predicament in which they become concerned with being evaluated through the lens of a negative stereotype, and which impacts performance and well-being. My students, colleagues and I are devoted to creating system-level interventions to combat stereotype threat effects.

I wince when pansexual cisgender guys compliment me on being the 'best of both worlds' – It's often a microaggression that equates gender with genitals – but in queering this phrase, I think, yes, many of us transguys could be the 'best of both worlds' if what that means is that we celebrate and learn from our female histories, be alert and accountable for our own sexist actions, call other men out on theirs, try our best to become one of the good guys, and in doing so, come home to ourselves with integrity and joy.

21

Today I Am a Man

By Evan R.
Age 44, Trans Male

[Editor Note: With the closest LGBT community being hours away from where Evan lives, he chooses to live quietly, and is not "out" as a trans man. He starts his story at the very beginning, and takes us through the various time periods of his life in order to highlight how being trans is not something that just "appears" out of nowhere. For most, in hindsight, the question or observance of gender and our preferences and/or incongruities was apparent before we were school age. In writing his story and his experiences, Evan embraced his truths and found his voice, and now shares with you in hopes of helping others along in their own journeys, and helping others to understand.]

※※※

Children are born innocent. They are born without choice, without malice, without knowledge of the world. We are all born that way, at least that's what I understand. Who is to know what hidden complexities of multiple factors come together to create the baseline of who we are as individuals. I did not choose these things though I have read that both gender and orientation are born with you; that at critical points in the womb, a fetus can be exposed to levels of sex hormones in the mother that can cause gender and/or sexual orientation to be different from the expected outcome. If this is true or at least to some extent true,

I can embrace that because I don't ever recall making a choice about either. As a child, I don't recall having prior knowledge of the kind of blatant and subtle sex and/or gender discrimination that can mar a life for years. Had I known, and gender and sex were, in fact, a choice I had to make at some point, I would never have chosen to be a lesbian, nor a trans male. As a child, all I wanted to be was loved, healthy and happy. Who wouldn't want that?

Background

My mother comes from a strongly Baptist background. Devoted to her faith she lived her life as an example of that faith. My father, on the other hand, came from a Catholic family. He never embraced any religious belief but attended church with my mother just the same. My mother trained as a nurse. My father started as an RCMP officer in the lower mainland but was later transferred as a Corrections Officer in Prince George. After a short time living in the city, my parents purchased a small, ramshackle cabin on thirty-six acres of agricultural land situated about twenty minutes south of town. It was there they became pioneers, so-to-speak. The community consisted of a small corner gas store surrounded by sprawling farms and rural 60s-70s housing that lined the main roads. Winters saw temps of -28° to -40° while summers could reach +25° C. Without hot water, electricity and in-house amenities, my parents managed to renovate the property, build a home, start a family, work full time and raise a menagerie of animals.

My Beginnings

In 1970, my older sister was born. She was full of life, talkative and independent. Nearly a year later, on a blistery, cold November day, I was born. My mom said I was a tiny, sensitive, quiet baby who came quickly into this world. I became the kind of child who needed to be near my mother, who cared about everything, who felt deeply about all things connective and organic. The natural world fascinated me. Though I did not say much, I took in all I could sense. My oldest sister was my voice for much of my growing up years. I looked up to her, as she was socially normal, smart, and was naturally respected.

Five years after I was born, my youngest sister came in to the world. At that time, my oldest sister and I were inseparable, best friends. My relationship with my youngest sister was complicated and temperamental. We got along fairly well, but at times, we became like ice and fire. We clashed. She was a brazen, spoiled child who defied respecting her older siblings and parents and seemed to get away with almost everything. Lee was prized as the older, wiser, more independent one. Interestingly enough, many years later our parents told us that they had always wanted a boy and fully expected that either the youngest or oldest would have been the son!

Though we all acted as tomboys – typical farm girls – I always remember being far more boy-like. I naturally, and nearly immediately, gravitated to what one might call "boys' stuff". I loved nature, getting dirty, having short hair, playing with trucks and sand and collecting toads and slugs in my pockets. I spent my days helping dad on the farm. I aspired to become like him, look like him, and do what he did. From a young age I assumed I was a boy, though I didn't actually know the difference. Dad and Mom never said a word to deter me from my natural understanding of things. They wanted to let us grow up without gender and sex pressures—none of this pink versus blue stuff. We were allowed to be ourselves. I am incredibly grateful for this.

Growing up for me seemed magical for a long time. It wasn't until I accidentally caught a glimpse of my father nude, sitting on the edge of his bed, that I realized he had something I didn't have—a penis. I didn't know what that was at the time but it started to confuse me then—I started to ponder, "*if I am so much like Dad, am Dad's son, why don't I have that thing and what is it?*" Then I started realizing that boys wear pants and shirts to church and I was wearing little dresses, like my sisters. My hair grew long and was combed fluffy and I carried a little purple purse with me on Sundays. When I started realizing marked differences between males and females and pronouns etc….my confusion started to flicker. At home, on the farm, I could be the little boy, Dad's son but at school and church and other places, I had to be a girl. I was back and forth like a yo-yo but my sisters, although tomboy-like as well, did not have to go between extremes. They seemed settled.

Entering the School System – Welcome Rejection

Living so far out in the country meant we did not often see other kids our age. On the first day at Kindergarten, I remember being so scared that I hid in the coat closet and cried after my mother dropped me off. Hours later, I went into the boy's washroom to pee, but got severely punished by the teacher and in front of the class. I was so embarrassed and confused. These would be the kids I would grow up with and now I was marked as "weird".

On top of that, I had a hard time learning in school, especially with respect to math and telling time. My niche certainly was gym and creating art. As primary school progressed and I became familiar with the kids, I began to identify more with many of the boys. I was disgusted, however, by those boys who were mean, aggressive, and potty-mouthed, those who fought others and poorly treated animals.

Over time, I drifted into the circle of boys who adopted me as one of them, but at the same time I started to be abhorrent to the girls. Some girls, the pretty, popular ones, started to bully me. As a safety measure, I clung to hanging out with the boys until they started liking girls. That was when they started to see me as being really weird. By that time I had been doing what they do, including checking out the girls, playing in the mud, being crazy on the tire swings, pinching girl's butts in class, and so on. By Grade 5, it was clear—I no longer fit in anywhere but at the family farm.

Not fitting in while already being a quiet, shy kid, made me even more antisocial, and that created a circle of rejection that started to stick. I learned to detest school, the bus rides home, and the way I was treated. To cope, I stayed quiet, cried myself to sleep at night, wrote dark poetry to older girls I had a crush on, got heavy into sports to feel stronger and worked harder on the farm. I was classed as a "low-lifer" by other school kids, so only a few, other low-lifer girls hung out with me. We stayed together to keep each other safe but even amongst them, I felt alien.

By Grade 7, I knew I was sorely different from the others. By then, I was so weird and antisocial, I was a target for anyone with a mean streak. At that time, I knew I was a boy, I always knew, but simply could not understand *why?* Why was I being treated like a girl, having to conform, and having to be bullied by them? Why were boys rejecting me? Why were teachers not stopping it? *What was wrong with me?*

Enter Puberty – The Stony Gavel

Then came puberty, like a silent, caped killer in the night. I was a late bloomer—and had no idea what that even meant until it started to happen. Puberty was the death sentence for me. Once my mom knew that I started having a period and that my chest was developing, she immediately told my dad to lay off the hard farm labour. She said it wasn't the kind of work for young girls. She started buying me really 'girlie' clothes, made me wear a bra, and use menstrual pads. What else could she do? I was a weird kid, too 'tomboy' now, and it wasn't showing itself as a 'normal' phase anymore. No, I was becoming *too* tomboy. Alarm bells were going off. I started wearing super loose clothing to hide my slowly growing breasts. My posture started to go, I started becoming obsessed with being muscular…as boy-like as I could become.

Puberty scared me. I started to develop a very sexually active mind from Grade 7 onwards. So bad that to vent I drew out on paper—people having sex—and then fantasized about it, wrote poetry about it and then, neatly folded the papers up and hid them under the base boards of my room. Like I really knew anything at all! To combat having to accept I was a female, I started stuffing my underwear with balled socks and fruit, just to see what it would look like if I had a penis and scrotum. When my family wasn't home, I would pack and feel so much better about it. I would constantly wonder about my father and what he looked like, how he functioned. Not only was I feeling more sexual, too sexual, it seemed, but I was getting deep crushes on girls older than I. Girls! I started to feel my maleness, though remained conflicted by what I didn't have.

At the same time, my parents were treating me differently—they started seeing me and treating me as a young woman. Distressed to the nth degree, I internally rebelled because I knew I was their son, but felt too scared to mention anything out loud. I remember my dad starting to talk differently to his male friends when I was around. It was as if they now had to watch their manners around me, whereas before, they saw me as dad's boy—his junior—and swore and talked the talk that guys generally do.

As my grades evolved, I became a loner who ended up losing myself in aimless, but highly emotional, sexual feelings I had for numerous girls. I also lost myself in soccer and competitive canoeing. My solace became nature—the back pond, the fields, the forests and wildlife. All of that never bullied nor rejected me. I felt understood in nature. Being forced to face a gender I knew I was not, and not being successful running from developing lesbianism, I started to crumble. I remember many nights, sneaking down into our basement to go through my mother's nursing texts to read everything I could get my hands on about sex, sexual organs and gender. After months of doing this, I figured I had multiple disorders and felt incredibly frustrated that this was all a very cruel joke that I couldn't be who I knew myself to be.

As my parents by this time ran a high end horse breeding business at the farm, it meant our stallions would have to "service" the mares. I remember my parents always having to shuttle us back into the house during this time. Once we got older, we were allowed to watch the mating process. I remember being both terrified at how rough and violent horse mating was, but, at the same time, I was fascinated by the male, by his huge member and how it worked. The disturbing visual of mating never left my mind; in fact, it fueled the sexual part of my mind. So I went into Grade 8 with all of this in my head.

Giving In

I don't exactly remember when it happened, but at some point in high school I succumbed to being a girl and a lesbian, and learned to lie to hide my weirdness. The last thing I wanted was for the bullies to have more ammo against me. In high school, my best friend ended up being a boy, an artist who developed a crush on me. At this time, I had fallen in love with girls so repeatedly that it seemed normal. Falling in love with a guy was odd for me in a big way. It made me feel like something was wrong. I did not like guys anyways—they made me feel like I was never equal to them, never strong enough, never guy enough...only a weak female.

Grades 8-12 came and went. The bullying intensified. I retreated into the library where I devoured books and studying, obtained good grades and became excellent in my chosen sports. I looked and acted incredibly androgynous, being built like a boy, strong like one, but small and quiet. In gym class, I refused to change in the open change room and shower with the girls. I felt so out of place with them. I just wanted to be with the boys where I knew I belonged. But even so, many boys acted anything but what I knew myself to be.

I was caught in-between genders. Feeling constantly hated, misunderstood, lonely and desperate for love and deeply frustrated, confused at what the hell I was, hating myself on a daily basis and hating my body. I tried unsuccessfully, many times, to end my life. Not being successful fueled a growing anger in me. My parents sent me to a Christian psychologist to see how they could help me. That ended up being a joke, because the guy just stared at me and concluded I was going through a phase. I was on suicide watch and my relationship with my parents continued to dissolve. I started to dislike them for forcing me to accept being something I wasn't, hating them for not understanding me, for having even created me.

When Grade 12 graduation came, my mom had a dress made for me. It was dark navy blue with white lace and my hair was all done up to the nines. I hated every minute of it. No one at school would care anyway. They were, however, shocked to see me when I arrived at the school because I looked so completely different from my usual androgynous self. It was not me though—in my view, I was a boy dressed as an awkward woman. My grad party was camping in the wilderness with my best friend, a girl I ended up having a huge crush on for nearly seven years.

Fast Froward to Pre-T

I lived at home until I had completed Grade 12 and eight months of leadership training at Calgary's, Baptist Leadership Training School. It was at this place I met my first girlfriend. Up until that happened, I stayed relatively quiet about being a lesbian. I went to this school to try to get rid of being a lesbian—to stop being sinful. Once my parents found out I had a girlfriend, my relationship with them and my older sister deteriorated. I left on bad terms and moved to the downtown core.

I moved in with one of the male leaders I had befriended at the family church, and lived with him until my girlfriend was able to move up from Vancouver. I lived with her for a few years, then went through multiple lesbian relationships and jobs in PG, obtained my BSc, worked for a while more, and then moved to Victoria to start my life over and to live with my older sister in 2001. I lived with her there for eight years before she went to Europe to get her PhD.

All this time, despite persistent longing to be me, I suppressed my maleness and continued to embrace lesbianism. Though I never quite felt I fit in with the community, I never quite felt like a lesbian, I didn't want to open my can of worms. It wasn't until several years after moving to Victoria that I came to face-to-face with myself.

Journey to Freedom

On one occasion in Victoria, I remember meeting a room full of women with beards and moustaches. I was immediately taken aback, confused at what these people were. Some had deeper voices and all acted very male. My reaction was "holy shit, I *really* don't fit in here!" and quickly left, never to return. To me, I felt horribly like I just witnessed a freak show. But, you know, that experience stuck with me and never left my mind.

I started an Environmental Technology diploma at the local college, and while there, I noticed a very tomboy-looking kid in my class. For the longest time I could not tell if the person was male or female. This person was quite popular and people seemed to really like them. As time went by I kept noticing this person and something started to happen—I started to sense a growing, seething feeling rise in me that flared up each time I watched them. Not sure what to make of this, I tried to avoid person x at all times but to no avail. Not sure at the time where this horrible, aching anger came from but it was bad and it started to affect me over time. I thought that maybe I was jealous that here is this masculine, attractive person who seems to relish being liked and seems quite out about it. Must be a dyke, I thought.

Then, one day, the school paper had run an article on the front page about a guy named Danny. A trans-guy. And there looking back at me was this person x. A "transgender" person still living with his parents, a person waiting to be old enough to be able to go on HRT, a person happy in a relationship with a woman at the local university. I was gobsmacked. Then my anger made a shift and turned to white ire. I knew at that point I was in pain and that this was a thorn.

It was about this time that I had started noticing certain people going to the college and realized they were sort of women, but had moustaches and beards. Then I realized who they were. My circus freak-based reaction was replaced by intense curiosity. Little did I know that exposure to these people would crack me open to my childhood roots that I had been trying to cover up and hide, even from myself. Danny reminded me of me, how I was back when I was in my early years. Here I was facing myself. Only this time, I heard there were options—hormone and medical options—to make things right.

Options! Options to change! What a concept! So instead of hating Danny and mulling over all my years of not being able to do anything and running from it anyway, I started to do research. Weeks and months rolled by and I found myself chest-deep in YouTube videos of people documenting their transition on HRT. I was absolutely floored.

Though I still felt absolutely alone in my torment, it was the research that kept me alive. The more I watched and read, the more I felt completely aligned, like I had somehow found my family. Now in my late thirties, I was facing myself. Angry that I didn't have the opportunity to change my outward appearance to meet who I am in the inside, angry no one seemed to notice, pay attention and help me. I was angry of all the things that went wrong in my life; the failed relationships, the low self-esteem, the fact I could not work sexually, my aversion to many things female etc. I was angry and bitter that now I am "old" and I had missed out on living my life fully as a boy, a teenager, a young man and now, an older man approaching his forties.

Then, I felt intense fear rise, fear that I am too old to be able to make a difference, fear that no one would accept me if I transitioned, fear of losing my family and girlfriend and friends, fear that I would never get a job and be shunned by the public, the church and ultimately, by God Himself, fear of becoming homeless or killed. It was bad enough I had been living as a lesbian for all my life, but to be trans now? That would be total suicide if I acted on it.

Yet, I could not ignore it either. In fact, now that the cat was let out of the bag, my entire being could not let it go. Soon I found a small group of trans men who met every other night. Despite being terrified of being rejected or not liking whom I meet, I went. Meeting those seven men, each going through some level of transition, changed the game for me. Upon reading Jamieson Green's book, reality hit me full in the face. They all helped me realize I can, indeed, do this. They made me feel like I had found family.

Eventually, I told my girlfriend, and she was very supportive. We made the trip to Vancouver to see a top gender therapist, and a four-hour assessment determined me to be a textbook case. I left with my emotions all over the place. I met a trans man running a sex shop in Vancouver and I picked up a binder. Was this really happening? I was overjoyed beyond belief, but still scared. Now I had to tell my family.

Upon returning home, I started to feel the enormity of the situation and all its uncertainty. Armed with a swath of information, I started to wonder if I was pushing myself toward transitioning, if I was becoming my own worst enemy and was allowing myself to be sucked into a fad that has so little research done on it. I started to question if I was being selfish. I mean, who was I to change what God made me to be? What are emotions, if they can be deceiving? Was it right to embark on a journey that I could never return from, that could end my life here as well my life afterward? How silly could I be to think I could seamlessly become a man in society, Even though I was already some kind of male used to being suffocated all my life, I was still a male. Would it be enough to "pass" to be "accepted" by other males? Would my girlfriend still want to be with me? Would I get stuck mid-way in transition and never really look male or female. Would I become a crotch-scratching, womanizing ass-hole of a man?

Oh, the questions! They kept coming. Eventually, they came so hard that I stopped my trans research altogether. The biggest worry I had was telling my parents—somehow I knew they would be hurt beyond repair.

Meanwhile, I waited for the gender therapist to get back to me on booking an endocrinologist for me. A year went by, and during that time I busied myself with trying to avoid all things trans-related. I finished school and work and started to think about moving to the Okanagan to be closer to my aging parents. October 2011 came, and my girlfriend and I travelled to see my parents for Thanksgiving.

It was there I started to succumb to bouts of panic and anxiety attacks I could not control. I started to hide them from my parents until my girlfriend noticed. I told her that I had to tell my family or I won't make it. I literally felt that I was going to die if I continued down this path of denial. The truth spilled out one night, but to my utter shock, my parents were fine with it. They eventually told me "Hey, let's get this thing rolling for you".

Now I can't ever say my parents have not been there for me. I have incredibly supportive parents who bend over backwards for their kids which is why I worried I would destroy them with my news. Telling them was the single most saving grace I have ever felt. Once that was out of the way and I saw a clear path to transition, I contacted my gender therapist. She gave me the go ahead to see another doctor in Vancouver who could prescribe me HRT.

I went to the All Genders Clinic on Commercial Drive and met a doctor so kind and genuine that I could have melted. She assessed me again, and had me meet a trans male nurse named Finn. I could not believe Finn was a trans male! Muscular, hairy, masculine body and face and deep voice—I was floored. He taught me how to use the syringe and T, and saw me off with a smile.

Shortly afterward, my girlfriend and I moved to a small house by a lake in Armstrong. On Nov 15th, 2011, after hours of anxious sitting on the chesterfield with a full needle in shaky hand, I took my first shot. Accomplishing that was pure joy. My girlfriend and I had told the landlords, prior to moving, that I would be transitioning there and they were welcoming of it.

So that is where my transition began. It happened slowly, even at 100 mg/kg every week. At many points I thought I must be intersex because no changes were happening. It was a time of apprehension and excitement. Then the voice started to crackle. I soon could not carry on a conversation without sounding like a Canada Goose. My girlfriend got a job, but I was unable to find anything until Spring 2012.

By that time, our relationship started to crumble. She started to have difficulty seeing me as a male but had a hard time to communicating that with me. I was indeed changing, and perhaps not to her liking. My voice got deeper and I started to bloat, a lot. Once hired by a provincial NGO, my name was still Erin. I was hired as a girl because I had not yet transitioned enough to pass as a male. The company did not know at first until I was hired. Out of anxiety about them finding out and firing me, I told my supervisor, who was absolutely fine with it. Our training took place at a fishing lodge. It was there I, with my crazy Canada goose voice and bloated body, met the company and employees, including the guy I would be partners with for the summer. None knew I was trans except my supervisor.

Once I told my summer partner, he was fine with it, in fact, he treated me like another guy all summer. We got along great. All that summer and into the fall I continued to stay bloated while my voice cracked. I was using mascara to darken all the light hairs on my face. No actual hair growth was occurring yet. It was good that at least he was fine with me transitioning. That summer and into fall, I managed to move between several bloat periods. But, soon enough, I started noticing my voice deepening, facial and leg hairs thickening and darkening along with other secondary male sex characteristics. I was ecstatic. Very soon I was able to use the men's washroom and be fully, as some would call it, "stealth" in society.

I was watching YouTube videos on topics that some guys were quite vocal about, such as "Not being trans enough" and "how to pass as male", etc. I found it challenging to agree with these topics. Even though I am transgender and pass 100% as a cis-gendered male in society I am by no means one to judge whether someone is trans-enough or not. The variation in how trans males feel and act, how they frame their trans understanding follows that of a true bell curve one would see in nature. There are extremes and large grey areas meaning that diversity is huge.

For me, I feel mostly male, and I don't want to be transgender, I just want to be male—whatever that is or looks like for me. I am by no means a subscriber of societal characterizations of what a male should be—tall, muscular, hairy, big phallus, strongly masculine behavior, lack of emotion and certain, or aggressive language. I mean, really, what makes a man a man, a woman a woman and every one in between valid enough to be who they are—they simply just *are*.

I think the better questions are how human one is, how compassionate one is, what one's morals and values are. Even then, it is still another bell curve. So, as I was transitioning, I was dealing with numerous adjustments that I felt I had to make without changing my personality and my baseline essence. Since I did not have the chance to grow up male through and after puberty, I did not really know how to act, what to say and how to communicate with others as a male. To me it was, and is, important, if for any reason, safety. I had to learn, and am still learning, how to work within society as a stealth trans man who wishes to remain that way.

To date, I feel I have assimilated fairly well despite not having a lot of hair growth and height! My confidence has increased and so has my belief in myself—two of the things I struggled most with in my pre-T life. That said, testosterone did not solve deep- seated, self-esteem issues and pseudo-antisocial behaviours and reactions which developed from years of being exposed to bullying and discrimination by both men and women. My transition has been fairly smooth—I feel lucky compared to the many trans people I have heard/read about and watched on YouTube videos.

Fast forward through the red tape of name changing, to navigating through the politics of getting a two-year temporary passport, to having a life changing chest surgery with Dr. Garramone in Florida. That surgery alone had a huge freeing impact on me. Months later, I had a cancer scare with abnormal cells in my cervix. That led to tests and eventually a full hysterectomy. Both surgeries left me with keloid scarring, something that many guys must deal with but, even so, I would not have avoided those surgeries. Now, four years later, I am working on obtaining bottom surgery in eastern Canada. Though I realize not all guys want bottom surgery, for me it is necessary. I am hoping to have this done in fall/winter.

Long, long story short, I am happy with my transition. Despite going bald and being small, I am lucky to have found a life-long partner who may become my wife in the near future. I am surrounded by loving friends and family, and employers who once knew me by my last name, have never judged me. Most others I know simply see me as 'that farmer guy.'

I still struggle with dysphoria and my faith of course—never fully knowing what God really feels about me changing his design. It is a constant, aching uncertainty I hope one day will be resolved. Rarely do I have an anxiety about whether or not I made the right choice. For me, there was no other realistic option. Transitioning has given me a new lease on life and I am embracing it. The magic of transitioning however, has lessened now. I have settled into fewer T-related changes and more age-related changes. Securing a strong, meaningful career and marriage are my main personal goals now. As an added bonus is the helping others where and when I can and…helping in any trans-related research, papers, what have you. I commend those people who are out there trying to make a difference for trans people.

My Community Now

I only know a few trans guys who are friends of mine. I live in a community that does not have GLBT outreach of any kind, and the closest support is in another city hours from me. My best support comes from my partner, parents and friends who know I am trans. That all aside, I honestly don't feel trans although I am. I feel like a regular guy living in society so don't feel the need to seek out trans community. It's not that I want to avoid being a part of the community, I just don't feel the need to be out about myself.

I have documented my transition on YouTube as others have done. The stories videotaped by many trans guys inspired and calmed me when I needed it the most so my videos were made in attempt to help others.

Over the years, I have been introduced to some trans guys pre-T who needed a big brother-like person in their life. It has been a complete joy being that person for them. They are now successful on their own and are transitioning smoothly. I wish I had that when I was starting down the path. But in my case, I needed older trans males to help me. Most guys I've met are younger and even nowadays, are even younger than that. So in a way, acting as a big brother for guys is my way of quietly advocating. I wish I could do more from my position.

22

Porn, Swing Clubs, and Bathhouses

By Lee Harrington
Age 36, Transman

[*Editor Note: This chapter contains sexually-explicit situations and language, and it may or may not be offensive or triggering for some readers. Lee's story is not unique, but it is unusual...and it is one that cannot be effective in sharing his truth unless he communicates it from the perspective of his own experiences. His story is not about sex; rather it is about men and objectification, and an atypical, yet healthy, method of looking at it all. Lee is not the only transman who has come from this type of experience, but he has chosen to educate others using his experiences, and has dedicated his life to doing so.*]

⌘⌘⌘

As humans, we each interact with the other in different ways – as friends, allies, enemies, family, frustrations, and passing acquaintances. Sexual touch and behavior is, of course, another way people also interact. Through transition, so much has changed, and so much stayed the same. This is what my journey has showed me.

In feminist theory, and my own queer interactions within women's community before my transition, one of the concepts that was vilified was the notion of consumption by the male erotic gaze. Men, it argued, needed to learn not to abuse the female form. This could begin with awareness being brought to the consciousness of men through decon-struction of how they observe, and objectify, women. Stopping visual abuse would transform how men treated women.

The theory is an overly simplistic one. Devoid of nuance, I still expe-rienced it. Not so much as experiencing that gaze as inherently violent, though those experiences happened. However, the erotic male gaze did simplify me down to being only a product. As an individual who has been part of the porn industry, swinger spaces, and bathhouses, I gained the benefit of viewing this experience from different gendered perspec-tives. Transition itself transformed my viewpoint as well, lessons learned with legs spread and nude before the world.

*

Bend over and let me see your ass. That's right, such a good girl. You like it, don't you. You want it.

The camera is rolling in a studio space in Los Angeles. Up a set of innocuous stairs and through the door, he asks me and my escort if we want anything to drink. Rodney Moore is an odd mix of sleaze and po-liteness, asking to see my tits and confirm that I am a fit for the project. *Scale Bustin' Babes* – how's that for a series title.

Based in the "chunky" category at size 14-16, the porn industry had a fascinating take on my look. Either I was chubby, or when corseted down to a 38D-28-42, a fetish queen. The take every producer had on me had nothing to do with me. I was an erotic cut-out to jam a cock in; a commodity to weigh out the value of, at least on set. Off-set, I loved a number of my producers. Great guys or gals. Mostly guys, whether ap-pearing in straight or lesbian work.

When I came out as trans, I was still working in the industry. With my head bald when genderqueer presenting, I donned a collection of wigs, becoming a chameleon. Blonde girl bound, brunette with a wicked grin, redhead with big eyes. One evening shook me to the core though.

This producer had worked with me for a number of years, making bondage and kidnapping themed films. He'd always been dubious on his safety skills in his portrayals of kink, though never enough to have me feel outright unsafe. Based in the Bronx, we were shooting at another producer's loft in Brooklyn. Due to the theme of his work, he wanted to shoot in stairwells, rooftops, hallways – all reasonable options. He had found out earlier that evening the news of my gender experience and plans to transition, as I and the other producer had been joking about using my tits to have them removed.

Disheveled, with my winter coat under me, I was tightly bound and gagged at the end of a hallway, near the fire escape. Dirt, garbage, and even a bit of broken glass made for a realistic set to transport the viewer to a place of dark fantasy. This being before my hysterectomy, it was that time of the month, though I tried to be mindful. My body had other plans, and I could feel a bleed-through coming on. I grunted three times and he paused the camera, asking me what was going on.

I told him. He threw the gag back in and told me that I must be some sort of freak then, because guys don't have periods or bleed. That I was mentally ill, and fuck me, he'd shoot me as long as he wanted to. I bled through, down onto the coat. I screamed at him to let me out. He just laughed.

No longer could I fit to his gaze. To the viewing gaze as a product. Therefore, I was worthy of abuse, a broken item in his eyes.

I ask myself, will this abuse be here for the rest of my life?

*

Oh yeah, babe. Gods you are so hot. Bend over and let me see that ass. I want you so bad.

I used to frequent swinger's spaces from time to time, usually coming with friends and lovers who enjoyed sexual adventure. Showing up as a pack, we could hunt together, play together, or have our own adventures before heading home together. It was a lark, a good evening out, quality time with quality people, or playful time with others.

Though the tiny girl and breast implant thin woman aesthetics tend to be popular to the male gaze in such spaces, there is space for almost any female body. Flirting in the social or dance floor, you meet someone and head upstairs. Watching a porn film side by side, one knee will graze another. Pressing legs further together becomes an affirmation of returned desire, while pulling your leg back is a statement of "not right now." The take each lover or voyeur had on me had nothing to do with me. I was an erotic cut-out to jam a cock in; a fantasy to weigh out the value of, at least at the club.

When I transitioned, I lost access to many swinger's spaces. Bisexual men are frowned upon in a wide number of swinger's clubs, with exceptions slowly popping up. But transmen and transwomen alike cause confusion to the heterosexual eye. If he has a beard but a cunt, am I gay? If she has breasts and a cock, am I gay? The second is often written off as a fetish experience, but the first is simply confusing in many clubs.

One exception, however, is *Power Exchange*. A swinger's club and erotic adventurer's playground in San Francisco, this grimy and gritty space is the sort of place that charged more to guys who wore street-wear. This led to dark and creepy spaces with nude men in tennis shoes, holding a towel, wandering around wanking at whatever caught their eye.

Many clubs have separate rates for women, men (in fetish wear, street wear, or nude), and couples. This lead to confusion with the trans patrons who frequented *Power Exchange*, which had become known as a bit of a t-girl meat market. Would people be gauged on wardrobe, identity, or legal gender? Thus, they added transgender to the list, letting all trans folk in for free. Simply declare you were trans and you'd get in, as they assumed you'd be naked soon enough to prove it.

Traveling alone, I had brought a Hitachi vibrator and stack of condoms with me. Plan for your own entertainment has always been my thought in most of life. Finding a small room that has a wall up that only goes to belly-height, voyeurs are able to wander by or watch, while still providing a modicum of privacy. Stripping down, I plugged in, positioned myself with my feet facing out, and went to town.

Having enjoyed myself thoroughly, I opened my eyes to find two guys standing a foot or two away. They were smiling, but perplexed. They had apparently paused to watch the girl with hairy legs masturbate, only to catch sight of my bearded face and flat chest. Confused, enthralled, they had to know more.

The next 30 minutes were a 101 class about transgender people, and trans men specifically. I was a curiosity under their gaze. A woman not a woman any more, a man they could still enjoy with their eyes closed – or open, if they dared.

They had to figure out how to consume me in their gaze. How to enjoy the product. I was worthy of respect only if they could make sense of me, as one of them even admitted that they had heckled "tranny freaks" in the past.

I ask myself, can we convert our oppressors one fuck at a time?

*

Oh yeah. Show me that ass. You want me to fuck you? Show me how much you want me.

An innocuous space off of Market street, *Eros* opens up to a small landing where you are carded, handed a locker key and towel, and sent on your way. With a social area and locker room downstairs, along with classic sauna and showers, it is beautifully up-kept. Upstairs leads to the winding maze of sex spaces and voyeur opportunities, as well as a massage therapist who does not offer happy endings.

Similar in some ways to the porn-viewing touch-response system from swinger culture, the world of bathhouses took a bit to get used to. Having been socialized female, and embedded in queer women's community as well, the systems of masculinity present take navigating. In women's sex spaces, there tends to be more conversation, for example.

This mirrors the overall bathroom experience difference between men's and women's restrooms. Complimenting someone's shirt while washing your hands is normal in the women's room. In the men's room, it's keep your eyes down and mind your own business. The first year in men's toilets led to a sorrow that was hard to place, a depression based on the idea that no one notices guys. Guys don't talk to other guys, at least in the world at large.

The sexual gaze and consuming experience changes that concept of noticing other guys. Instead of flirting and talking on the dance floor, cruising is the language at play. Look. If they catch your eye, look away, and look back. If their eyes are still there, this is an opportunity to connect. Because of cruising culture, people appraise from a distance. They also appraise by touch, a hand moving to a stranger's ass to see if you like what is there, and they like what you are offering.

Through these layers of appraisal, a potential lover might turn away at any moment, or come forward for more. The take each guy had on me had nothing to do with me. I was an erotic cut-out to jam a cock in; a possibility to weigh out the value of, at least in the bathhouse.

During my first trip to a bathhouse, I took this all personally, or assumed it was because no one wanted a trans guy. Even though I was at the bathhouse that hosts a M for FTM night. A realization struck that indeed, each male gaze is a different one. Some men would be seeking twinks, some bears, some black men, some Latino boys. I was just another commodity.

Suddenly I felt less alone under the male gaze. I had acquired the male gaze, for I too had been empowered with the tool to gaze upon other, consenting, men. There was a balance in power present in the experience, because suddenly we were all equally oppressed.

I don't fit into some of their gazes. But am still viewed as a product. Therefore, I could join in this patriarchal practice, not any more broken than anyone else.

I ask myself, is this act of consumption so bad?

*

Look at that ass. How sexy. I wish I could touch it. My gods they are hot.

When I transitioned, I tracked my mental and physical changes intently. My tastes in food transitioned – I like mustard more. My sense of smell – I'm convinced it's the only way men can tolerate men's rooms. Even my ability to watch violence changed with me– I never used to have the capacity to watch the Saw movies without having nightmares.

Sitting in Sydney one afternoon with my former partner, we were eating gelato at a little place on King Street called *Gellatomassi*. The day was beautiful, with sun streaming down, as I gazed out into space. "What are you looking at?" he asked, and I snap out of it, into a place of simultaneous shock and shame. Apparently I had been staring, my head turning to follow, a denim-clad ass.

I can't say if the ass belonged to someone male, female, or otherwise identified. I can't tell you if they were trim or rotund. I can only say that it was a denim-clad ass. The take I had on them had nothing to do with them. They were an erotic cut-out to jam a cock in; a desire that I unconsciously was weighing out the value of, at least in that moment.

Never in my life had I objectified in a way that was truly, well, objectifying. I'd treated people as a hot lover to enjoy for a night and set aside. I'd enjoyed people as one-dimensional parts of themselves. But they were always people.

Not this person. They were an ass. It was an ass. There was not even a "they" in the conversation. My shock and shame turned into horror, sorrow, and finally, fascination. As a transman raised by a strong feminist, I had been gifted with an analysis of the male gaze, an academic understanding of the male gaze. I had been in the male gaze, but until then, had never been *in* the male gaze.

This was not about men not having been socialized female, or been brought up as bad men. I had been brought up as a strong and powerful woman, with a window in my teens of attempting to transition and being turned down, entirely supported by that strong woman. I understand how simplifying people down to being nothing but a commodity is dehumanizing, especially in non-consensual situations. How it leads to abuse, and worse, taking people from having the rights of humans.

And yet, here the moment was. And it returns, unbidden. I catch it now – catch it, note it, and move on (with apologies if appropriate).

Does this notion give permission to the phenomenon of the objectifying male gaze? No, especially not when it causes harm. But it did create a sympathy for the behavior, an understanding of where the seed perhaps grows from.

What will fit into my gaze? To my viewing gaze consuming a product. Setting a good standard of behavior for other men. Not just of gazing with honor and integrity, but with personal understanding of the ramifications left from the rancid gaze.

I close my eyes, and gaze inward.

23

In New York You Can Be a New Man

Maxwell Alderdice
Age 30, Transgender Man

[Editor Note: Sometimes, it isn't the lack of language to explain how we feel, it's the absence of context. Maxwell first found comfort in the lesbian community, yet something was missing, hidden from his conscious thought. When the realization struck, he jumped in with his whole being. Viewing his life in the perspective of literature and theater has given him a new understanding of himself as he begins to close the curtain on the loss of his former connections, and has begun paving the way towards his new life and new connections.]

⚮⚮⚮

In New York City in late 2015, you could offer up an arm and a leg and still not receive tickets to *Hamilton*, Lin-Manuel Miranda's hip-hop opera about the titular Founding Father that had seized feverish hold of Broadway. In early August, soon after the show opened on Broadway, I enjoyed the fruits of my father's foresight instead of making such a sacrifice. A lifetime theater aficionado, he had snatched three tickets months earlier when murmurs of the show's future popularity first surfaced. In the back of the Richard Rodgers Theatre, my parents and I plunged into musical rapture as the opening number snapped to life. It concluded with the young Alexander Hamilton on a ship to New York City from his West Indian origin, the ensemble singing out around him:

A Herstory of Transmasculine Identities

In New York you can be a new man.

Almost two years earlier, New York had helped me become a new man. There were no LGBT health clinics in New Jersey where I lived, so I traveled into the city to visit Callen-Lorde Community Health Center. There, I received injectable testosterone to begin the physical transition from female to male.

In my limited knowledge of the world, I had never heard of composer-singer Michael Callen, but I knew who Audre Lorde was. I had spent fourteen years—half my young life at the time—identifying as a lesbian. She was one of the brave women I had once been able to claim an invisible connection with, a proud bond to someone who never knew I existed.

And now—?

Nearly two months after I saw *Hamilton*, the soundtrack released, and the rest of the world finally glimpsed some of the experience I'd savored in that theater. Swathes of the internet, where I spent most of my time and socialization, lit up with frenetic devotion. My own mind buzzed with lyrics.

I started reading the biography that inspired the musical—*Alexander Hamilton* by Ron Chernow. Every page was a strange shock as I compared and contrasted it to the more historically loose musical, which had, of course, sought to create a brilliant narrative rather than a truthful account. One thing stood out.

The musical depicted Hamilton surrounded by colorful friends, embedded deeply within the communal fabric of the young United States. His moments of solitary melancholy were intense but fleeting. The swiftly roaring, tight-packed show simply didn't have the time to include anything more. The book, though—in the book, while Hamilton was indeed an integral part of the Revolutionary War, he was also perpetually an outsider by virtue of his birth, and he felt it keenly. Depression and misanthropic feelings of isolation gripped him.

I, too, had grown up struggling with anxiety and depression from a young age, my life constantly sabotaged by it. Now, I look back and wonder just how much of it was gender dysphoria. Not all of it; both my parents had family histories of mental illness. And there's no point in dwelling on my past too much. It's too easy to become bitter and self-shaming over how long it took me to—

To do what?

I turned thirty in September of 2015. I wasn't fully through transition (are we ever fully through transition?), as I still needed to legally change my name, but I had been taking testosterone for a year and a half. Almost every stranger read me as male. More importantly to me at the time, I was in the last stages of preparing to finally move out on my own.

My parents' household had been terrible for me for a long time. My father was an intermittent alcoholic with a history of becoming verbally abusive when drunk, and my mother a deeply neurotic woman struggling with her own anxieties. My father's behavior was particularly bad when I was a teenager, which had left me feeling trapped and isolated.

That was when I came to realize my attraction to women, at fourteen. Although I participated in little activism and attended few groups, I found a sense of belonging in sharing part of my identity with other outcast women who boldly held onto their true selves in the face of adversity. I sought out every lesbian and bisexual female author I could find, relishing the social thread that bound me to these great women. I took comfort in knowing that my attraction to women was something sacred.

My realization of my sexuality was a lightning bolt. The electrical energy for it built up over a single summer of reading fantasy books with gay characters and staring at pictures of Bernadette Peters in the liner notes for *Into the Woods*. Fourteen years later, my realization of my gender identity was an earthquake: a shattering movement born from years of underground stress, which toppled everything I had known. Yet the places things fell over into made more sense than before. Except for one thing—where was my community now?

I came face to face with transmasculine invisibility. Mainstream society assumes it's *natural* for those classified as women to futilely wish to be male, because men are the ideal. Strangely, lesbian feminism doesn't challenge this assumption, merely adds to it: it's natural for us to wish to be male, because of internalized misogyny, but it's virtuous to defy that desire by holding onto our femaleness, or at least resisting maleness. Against this milieu, transgender men disappear like chameleons.

In that way, the truth of my own identity disappeared inside my mind for decades. It was still there, though, like stagehands in the wings of a Broadway show, quietly providing props for my inner angst. More and more, as I grew older, I felt trapped in a stifling present that dead-ended before reaching the future. I could not see myself thriving as an adult woman, and I didn't know why.

Midway through an early song in *Hamilton*, the protagonist declares, "For the first time I'm thinking past tomorrow." It's a line that resonates with me. The same thing happened in my life when I at last understood that my future was not that of a woman after all.

After a lifetime of dismissing all the signs as eccentricity and internalized misogyny, I accepted myself, but that didn't make everything that came after easy. I was a new man with all the same troubles of the old, along with the new distress of shifting from a proud community to a position of disconnection.

As transgender men, we have no guide, no narrative of our own. After I realized I was a lesbian, I read *Annie on My Mind, Rubyfruit Jungle, Oranges Are Not the Only Fruit*. I had nothing like that when I realized I was a man—only friends to talk to. I had no guidelines for resolving my struggles with my new identity. Was I one of the dreaded straight men now? Was it all right for me to identify as bisexual when I had considered myself lesbian before despite some lesser attraction to men, or was that just an attempt to cling to queer cred? I didn't know. I couldn't figure it out. Maybe I still can't.

Women are expected to bond and form communities with each other. Men are expected to go it alone. It's just one of many poisonous assumptions that we haven't done enough to challenge, thrown into stark relief for me by the contrast with the lesbian community I had always found solace in. For the most part, the break was easier for me because my queer connections were mostly online and in spirit. But, in some ways, that made it worse, because my image of "lesbian community" was so idealized. I only occasionally saw the infighting, the transmisogyny, the ugly politicking. The show I saw was one of solidarity.

As I began my transition, I wrestled with the closing of the curtain on that show. In the reality beyond it, though, I was not as alone as I feared. I had friends who would support me, many of them also grappling with questions of gender identity. This group may have lacked the mystique of a broad-ranging lesbian unity, but it was real, and the people in it would support whatever choices I made about my identity.

Shortly after my thirtieth birthday, I saw another excellent musical: *Fun Home*, based on Alison Bechdel's memoir. There's another name that needs no introduction to many lesbians. I read the book too, and I was struck painfully by the thread of Bechdel's desire for maleness throughout her story. She had the same personal ideal as I did, it seemed, and yet in the face of that, she remained a woman, a butch lesbian, and made a name for herself in that community.

I couldn't do that. It takes me a long time to realize what I need to do in life, but once I do, I go through with it fast and with a whole heart. Once I knew my inner landscape was male, I had to take hold of my outer life and rearrange it to reflect that. If I lost my proud and invisible connections to other (or rather, I know now, *Other*) women as a result, if I had to discard my defiant purity to taint myself with patriarchy, I accepted that with some pain.

And what did I gain?

Lin-Manuel Miranda's musical depicts a gritty but brilliant Revolution, whirling brightly around the well-connected figure of its protagonist. Ron Chernow's book depicts a man who would always, despite his excellent connections, be on the outside on some level. In the end, though, Miranda's work is a beautiful fiction, and Chernow's is as close to reality as we can get centuries later. Fiction stays captive on the stage, playing out the same story night after night. Reality progresses forward.

In early October of 2015, I took my luggage and my cat and got on a plane that would bring me to my new home in the suburbs of Seattle. I was already a new man at that point. I had my own community in the form of the friends I had kept throughout my transition. That was real. So was this: The old me, unconsciously hiding behind a female mask, would never have stepped onto this plane. Whatever I had lost, I could move forward now.

24

Being Myself

By Caden Rocker
Age 32, Non-binary/FTM

[Editor Note: From being a lesbian to being a heterosexual man...from lesbian couple to heterosexual one... Caden asks a thoughtful question "At what point did I stop being a lesbian?" He shares his navigation of gender with its various identities and expressions when he had no concept or context of transgender, then later finding a way to reconcile himself with his own philosophies, rather than continue to be put into boxes imposed by other trans people.]

※※※

Gender identity and sexual orientation are two different things, yet society seems to intersect the two in many ways. I was a Girl Scout, I played softball, basketball, and field hockey, went to Lilith Fair, and never remember enjoying wearing dresses. When I came out to my mother as a lesbian when I was in high school, she wasn't surprised when I finally gathered myself enough to tell her; the only response was to ask something along the lines of "is that all you had to say?" I never thought I would find myself coming out to her again as my true self, preferring to be viewed/identified as male/masculine instead of the "daughter"/female she gave birth to. Coming out to my mother as identifying as someone who is Trans was a lot different than when I told her that I was lesbian, and seems to be an ongoing process.

I was married as lesbian and then divorced while being perceived as the male in a heterosexual couple; where does that leave me now? If I go shirtless now, the rainbow pride triangle tattoo I have will make people think I'm a gay guy, yet I got it when I was a proud lesbian and never thought I would be walking around in public without a shirt on because I had breasts. When I came out to my mother as being a lesbian, I was not aware of the broad spectrum of gender identities that exist. I had always been somewhat of a "tomboy" growing up, and I remember at least one time as child being told I was going into the wrong bathroom when entering the women's room.

There was sense of belonging, community I found in being a lesbian, even when living in a small city; yet now, with my beard and breast-less chest, I don't think I would be welcomed or feel like I belonged in a lesbian bar. Towards the start of my gender-identity journey I lost friends who were lesbians, as they saw my wanting to identify and "pass" as a male, I was "selling out" and that I was "giving in" to the patriarchal society that is disrespectful of women or those who are more feminine.

At what point did I stop being a lesbian? When I changed my name? Started testosterone? Was it changing the gender marker on my driver's license from F to M? Was it when I had a hysterectomy? Or was it recently, when I was finally able to have my breasts removed after waiting for years? After my divorce, I've continued seeing women. All of a sudden instead of being a part of a lesbian couple, I'm viewed as the male part of a straight couple, yet I still have my gay pride tattoo and my attraction towards women has never changed.

Even with being lucky enough to travel as a child, and growing up in a small, one-stoplight town in upstate NY, by my early twenties I had never even heard the term 'Transman'. The only representation of Gender Variant individuals that I saw growing up was from shows like "Jerry Springer". I remember watching a documentary that featured both a Transgender Women and a Transgender Man, and it was like a bolt of lightning went through me in some way. I took time exploring my feelings, seeing a therapist, reading, and realized that I did not identify as female, nor did I ever really fit in that box.

When I started my journey towards understanding my true self—who I am at my core—there were a number of opinions that I found. Many within the transgender community seemed to have certain ideas about how an individual should transition, and what one must do to "pass." I heard from numerous people that I needed to have top surgery and a hysterectomy right away along with starting Testosterone. I was told by many in online "support" groups and other environments that I would need to walk, talk, act "like a man," which seemed to involve taking up more space, acting more assertive and aggressive, and not showing emotions—at least not any "sensitive" ones. Early on, I remember constantly being worried about whether or not I was "passing," and being frustrated with the time it took for changes to come from starting testosterone. It seemed like I had finally figured out a huge, missing piece, and all I wanted was to make myself whole again; yet, instead of a single, large missing piece, there were many small pieces that would be needed to put together over time.

I still remember getting my first shot of testosterone, it didn't go as planned, but not much seemed to. I unexpectedly ended up going alone for my first shot of testosterone, and I still feel the sting of the needle as it plunged into my muscle for first the time. After the first shot, and the shots afterwards, something felt different, yet *right,* in my body like it was meant to have testosterone. I know there were subtle changes that started shortly after my first shot, but, for me they could not come fast enough. I remember waiting for my voice to drop, and for facial hair that needed to be shaved.

When I first started "transitioning," it seemed there was a clear start and end point with the main things being Hormone Replacement Therapy (HRT), and having Top Surgery to remove breasts that felt like they never belonged there in the first place. Last year, after over eight years of waiting, I was able to finally have top surgery completed, which was unexpected and life changing in so many ways. I knew in waiting that I would be so grateful to eventually be able to have top surgery, as the majority of insurances do not cover the procedure. Each year, I would hope and think this HAS to be the year, yet the years seemed to swim by with no shirtless summer in sight.

Before a few years ago, I would not go anywhere without a binder on, as I felt worried I wouldn't "pass." For over 2000 days, I wore a binder to work, to the gym, out to dinner, a quick trip to the store, and even in what was my own "home," I would have a binder on depending on who was there. I hated having to put on a binder every day, as it was uncomfortable and caused pain, especially after a long day's use, which was usually about thirteen hours. Yet, I loved my binder—it felt like a shield or my super hero uniform under my clothes; with my binder on, I felt like other people could see ME more like I saw myself.

A few years ago, after working with a good therapist and realizing the negative impact that wearing a binder was having on me physically, I stopped wearing my binder unless I was swimming. It was amazing to be able to go places without feeling so constricted yet I was always worried. I would be afraid that someone would somehow be able "to tell" and I always felt uneasy and anxious in certain spaces like a public bathroom. Sometimes, I would feel I had to wait until I could find a "safe" bathroom, and always felt I had to watch over my shoulder in gender binary segregated spaces. When I would go to swim laps at the gym I was always worried that I wouldn't "pass" despite having my binder and rash-guard on, and would always change in a bathroom stall.

In the time leading up to, and especially after all the change and processing of having Top Surgery, I feel like there really never is no clear start or end to this "transition," and instead consider it a Journey that is ongoing. Even before having top surgery, I did not have any real issues "passing," especially once I was able to grow a beard. Unless I or someone else has told someone that "I am Trans," they do not know, and the most frequent response when they find out is "I had no idea." Of course, there are the "coming outs" that I feel are necessary—like with new healthcare providers, significant others, and friends, and it, at times, can take thought not to accidently "out yourself." For example, looking at me and seeing a "white man" and then hearing me say something about being a Girl Scout when I was younger or that I played softball in school can cause a confused look or two.

In the wrong place, wrong time, or to the wrong person having my Gender Identity disclosed can put my safety at risk, and in many ways it would be safer to try to live "stealth." To me, however, trying to remain "stealth" about my Gender Identity Journey does *not* feel like I am able to be my *true, authentic self*. When I'm talking to a friend, I don't want to worry about whether I say Girl or Boy Scout when talking about my childhood. When I'm with My Lover, I want to know they are with Me for Me, not my Gender Identity.

I have no control over how someone processes my Trans status, whether they have known me for a year or my whole life. I feel lucky that I have never been physically attacked for expressing my true gender identity—for *being myself*.

25

The Most Important Lesson
From My Transition

By Max Meyer
Age 23, Transman

[*Editor Note: Max was fortunate, he was able to transition at a young age, which means he has the opportunity to view life from a slightly different perspective, since his adulthood begins with him living as his authentic gender. Max takes a look at life after-transition in order to highlight the fact that life circumstances still exist after transition.*]

There is a misconception that transitioning will fix all of the problems in your life. Although it does offer a great sense of fulfillment through the joyful acceptance and expression of a huge part of your identity, there are still other parts of your being to explore.

There is a void in every person, a sense of inadequacy, a doubt in the purpose of your existence. People have found a variety of ways to fill this void: alcohol or drugs, food, technology, career, exercise, religion or spirituality, and many lovers or a single person that defines their existence. Even though transition quiets the persistent voice saying something is wrong with your body, transition cannot fill that void either.

In the beginning of transition, I was so ecstatic. Everything was so new and exciting. I experienced the greatest relief to finally reveal my real self. There were so many little bursts of happiness to enjoy: the acceptance of old friends, hearing my new name, and seeing my new name in print. I took immense pride in every accomplishment along the journey. The transition happened quickly and relatively smoothly. I could not be more excited about my new life.

I struggled with the concept of divorcing from my past, personified in the old me. The idea of having a new life completely separate from the traumas of my childhood appealed to me: a new name, a new gender, a new chance in life. Transition can easily give life a new meaning and purpose.

Dread of the impending end of this happiness plagued me. I feared I would suddenly fall into the same old pit of despair. Instead, I slowly became aware of the old emptiness. The feeling of lacking something important still existed in my new life. This is not to say I regret my transition. I have a deep love for my body since transition. I am much more comfortable with myself and more confident. I would never go back to the person I was. When I completed my transition, I experienced the satisfied deflation that I feel every time I finish writing a book, end a relationship, explore my inner feelings, or accomplish a long-term goal. Transition is another project into which I have put a piece of myself. I invested a huge amount of time and emotion into discovering and expressing my gender identity. It is an experience that will affect many aspects of my life for the rest of my days.

I began to wonder what is the meaning of life past transition? What else can give me little bursts of happiness and pride? Will I ever be complete? Is the whole purpose of life to do well in school so I can get a good job so I can afford to put my own children through school? This cycle seems pointless to me. I want something more.

People have a misconception that since I transitioned at a relatively young age, I have answered all of life's questions. Yes, I have deconstructed society's notions of gender norms; explored the core of my identity, found the words to express myself, educated many people, and waged war against entire bureaucracies of medical corporations, school districts, and even the United States government, but that does not mean I know what to do with my life. There is not much written about what happens after transition.

Transition can consume your life. There will be hours spent exploring with psychiatrists, negotiating with doctors, and standing in line at courthouses and government agencies. There will be long, difficult conversations with family members, friends, employers, and teachers. You will feel certain that if you must defend your pronouns one more time to another ignorant person, you might explode. There will be times when you feel like you are drowning in the paperwork, not to mention hours of endless loops of aggravating hold music on the telephone. Soft classical music will slowly drive you insane. There will be days when you must battle your fears to leave the safety of your own home or to enter a public restroom. You will experience the brightest joys and darkest despairs. The emotions will enlighten your soul. All of these processes will devour so much of your time, expenses, mental power, and patience that your transition will become a second job, but transition is not an identity. Once everything on your checklist is completed, what will you do with your life? What will your next adventure be?

At some point, you will be faced with the same questions that everyone must answer—what do I want to be when I grow up? Where do I want to live? What do I like to do for fun? With whom do I want to spend my life? If the process of transition has consumed your identity, you will not be able to answer these questions.

This is why it is important to maintain a life outside of transition. Hobbies and social groups are crucial. Other goals, aspirations, and passions are critical. There is a lot to be passionate about when it comes to your gender, but life offers many additional passions. Although the process of transition may take years, you will eventually complete it. At which point, you need to be able to say, "I am enough. This life will be enough." Only then, will you be able to fill that void permanently.

26

My Gender—Both a Blessing and a Curse

By Tristan Rounkles
Age 25, Transman/Male

[Editor Note: Tristan shares his thoughts on the aspects of transition that not everyone thinks about when they begin their journey. Some people step into their transition journeys thinking it will solve everything—they are certain that once their bodies are in alignment with their mind, their problems will go away and life will be easier. For some, it does get easier in many respects, for others, the things they were trying to get away from are still there, and for others, the initial issues disappear only to be replaced with different ones. One aspect of transitioning when a part of the lesbian community that some don't always realize is that there is a high likelihood they will be ostracized from that community. Another is the fact that statistically, there is a good chance one will lose family and/or friends once they begin transition. Yet another facet of transitioning that changes is the status one has in society. Although already at the disadvantage of being seen as a woman, during those first weeks or months of a physical transition while waiting for testosterone to do its job, suddenly one has to think about which bathroom to use, what name to use for employment or legal documents, and dealing with the bureaucracies of medical and insurance providers, just to name a few of the myriad of frustrating, fearful or sometimes shaming obstacles one must traverse.]

❦❦❦

My birth certificate states that I am Holly Ann Rounkles, a female at birth. This is true for any other form of identification that has been assigned to me; however, these documents are merely a shell of who I am. I am not Holly Ann Rounkles, a female. My name is Tristan Christopher Rounkles and I identify as a male.

I came out to myself two and a half years ago, in 2013. Shortly after, I came out to those around me. Coming out to myself was the most challenging task I have ever accomplished, even more difficult than coming out to others. I hated myself and felt disgusted longer than I would like to admit. Eventually, I learned to accept myself and love myself. I conquered the hate, shame, and fear with self-talk every day. I told myself that this would get easier, that I am so strong, and that I deserve the happiness that I would find along the way and at the end of the rainbow.

On many occasions, I have been asked about when I first "knew" that I was a male living in a female's body. The question is never easy to answer, simply because there is more than one answer. It could have been around five years old when I would want to shave my face just how my father did. It could have around eight when I decided that dresses looked terrible on me. The most accurate answer would be that I have never truly felt female, so I somehow always knew. Sad, but true, is that I struggled with my gender identity and sexuality for nearly twenty years before I felt comfortable, and felt *me*.

My life has always been complicated, and adding my transition to the mix has made it even more so. Every day, I am learning about myself, the world around me, and to whom I matter the most. I used to identify as a lesbian, and most of my friends were lesbians. After beginning my transition, I realized that I actually identify as pansexual. I also realized that most of those lesbian friends do not enjoy being friends with a transgender male. The friends I acquired that did seem to enjoy being my friend did not understand how to differentiate me from a butch lesbian. Small story short, I had to distance myself. They did not understand that I am a male, which means that I do not enjoy lesbian exclusive bars or clubs; I also do not enjoy make up or getting my hair done.

To get into the sexuality side of my transition, it was hard for me to accept that I was pansexual. At first, I continued to date lesbians. This was no easy feat, especially not in the delicate stage of the first year of transitioning. I felt self-conscious, felt as though I was untrue to myself, and felt as though I was still perceived as a female. Eventually, I came to terms with the fact that I would only ever feel comfortable dating a cis-gender female who was pansexual, or a transgender female who was pansexual.

I am offended when others perceive my partner and I as a "lesbian couple," but it is something I will have to learn to deal with until I am able to pass as a male more days than not. I have been trying to accentuate my masculine features and attributes to fit in better with males, since I am still pre-surgery and pre-testosterone. Luckily, I was born with higher levels of testosterone, so I have male pattern facial hair in some spots on my face. I alternate between layering, wearing a binder, and wearing baggy shirts. I have adopted a male walking habit. I keep my hair cut in a more masculine way rather than a butch lesbian way. I make sure my face is shaven to avoid any peach fuzz growing where my facial hair does not grow in thick. Eventually, I will be able to afford top surgery, which will ease some of the confusion.

Aside from feeling like an outcast in the lesbian community, I have felt outcast from my old friends and family. For example, still to this day, some refer to me as "Holly," even though they know I prefer Tristan. Unfortunately, I have had to slowly let go of these relationships because they are doing more harm than good to my life. My ears ring, my heart pounds, and it is yet another reminder that I was not born a genetic male when I hear "Holly" coming out of someone's mouth. I have asked, demanded, and given time for respect, but sometimes it is a lost cause. As much as it has hurt to pull away from these relationships, I have learned to pick up, move on, and focus my energy on myself and the positive people in my life.

I was never warned that it would be difficult to keep friends or family around. I cannot exactly expect my siblings to let go of their sister and accept their brother. Nor can I expect my nieces and nephews to understand that their aunt is gone and they have a new uncle. Sadly, I was never able to come out to my parents, since they passed away before I even accepted myself. I have a feeling that they knew I was a male, though. My father bought me kid toy razors so that I could "shave" my face with him. My mom bought me boxers instead of underwear when I asked. They let me express myself as who I was, rather than what gender I was born into. For this, I will be forever thankful.

I will not forget the day that I looked into the mirror and realized that who I saw did not match the expectation of society. On this day, I saw a handsome man who was hiding beneath fear, hate, and shame. I realized then that I used to dislike being around guys because I was jealous of them. I was jealous of their bodies, facial hair, parts, and ease of attracting women. This realization helped me understand all of my feelings that I had bottled up for over a decade. I now know that I felt like a more effeminate male than female, because I really was one.

Every aspect of my life has been forever changed since I have come out as a transman. It's not exactly easy to tell your OBGYN who gives you a pap smear that you are transgender and would prefer male pronouns and your real name. Going to work is hard most days, because I haven't come out to everyone that I work with. Even using the bathroom has been a challenge, especially because I still have breasts, but I also have facial hair. Every day I struggle with being transgender, and I have come to terms with my identity being both a curse and a blessing. Some days I feel as though I have taken one step forward and two steps back.

I would have to say that I am very fortunate, though. I have finally discovered who I am. I have learned and become more courageous these last few years. Nothing in this world could replace the love, respect, and understanding I have for myself. I know that there are many more challenges I may face until the whole world views me as a male, but I know that I will be there eventually. The fact that I believe in myself and love myself, that my partner loves me for who I truly am, and that my handful of friends and family accept me for who I am, well, that is enough for now.

I never gave up on myself and I have overcome the loss of friends, family, and my previous identity. If you believe in yourself, you can overcome any struggle.

27

My Night In Drag

By L.W. Lucas Hasten
Age 50, Man

[*Editor Note: Lucas wrote in Chapter 11 that Drag is a performance, not an identity, and it is not uncommon for those who perform to use drag as an intermediate step toward transitioning to male. Although he was not a performer, Lucas was a lesbian feminist who is now an anthropology professor who still holds his feminist values close to his heart. The following is his account of an unforgettable evening of an eye-opening performance in the streets of New York, long before he transitioned into the man he is today.*]

※※※

Back when I was a woman, I became a man for a little while. Less than an evening, really. There are many who would have said, upon looking at me, that I already looked like a man, what with my short hair and sensible shoes, but I identified as a woman at the time. Then I underwent a complete transformation, as disturbing as it was sublime.

I knew it would happen eventually. I was writing my master's thesis about a group of drag kings in New York City who insisted unanimously that I couldn't do the subject justice without trying it myself. Yes, I said, it's true: I'm a buttoned-down shirt and boxers type of woman, but I've never intentionally tried to pass myself off as a man. It's one thing when people make the mistake on their own; it would be quite another if I set out to deceive them. We all knew all along that I was dying to do it. My biggest fear was that I might enjoy it a little too much.

The drag kings took it seriously. If you're going to be out in public, they warned, you'd better be passing. The last thing you want is to be recognized as a woman; people can get pretty crazy if they think you're messing with them. Swishy men aren't safe either, so you'd better practice walking. When you're a woman, you swish, no matter how butch you are -- a fact I was hard pressed to accept. I had to overcompensate.

The drag kings were full of advice. Take up a lot of space, they told me. Sit with your legs apart. Stand solidly. Walk slowly, heel to toe, in long strides. Make sure you wear men's shoes, because women's shoes are obvious. Don't smile. Try not to talk too much. Do everything you can to project an impenetrable aura of masculinity. Spitting, interrupting people, cutting in front of others in line -- all of these things say "MAN" in big bold letters. When all else fails, adjust your package.

The fateful night arrived and I bound my breasts with duct tape. If this sounds like a good idea, read it again: I bound my breasts with duct tape. I voluntarily endured the equivalent of a six-hour mammography. I was wearing a T-shirt under the tape, of course, but that did little to ease the discomfort of having my nipples strapped under my armpits. The one bonus was all of the extra space it afforded me behind the steering wheel of my car.

I combed my hair straight back with gel and took off all of my earrings. I had bought a nice checked shirt for the occasion and a colorful tie; the shirt was fine but my neckwear was dismissed in favor of a morose little brown number with blue diagonal stripes, the sort of tie boys wear in a junior high class photo. I topped off my ensemble with a packer, which can be loosely defined as anything you put in your pants to make people think you have a penis. No, I don't mean a fat wallet. In my case, I stuffed a sock inside a sock inside my underwear, my costumer admonishing, "Don't make it too big. Everything looks bigger under clothes!" It didn't feel like much, but it made a convincing enough bulge.

Using clippings of theatrical hair and spirit gum, we put a very reasonable mustache on my upper lip and a smart little jazz beard in the divot between my lower lip and chin. It's funny what a little facial hair can do. People don't see your tits anymore. Dress the right way and BAM! - instant man. When I looked in the mirror I laughed out loud. I was a large woman, so I made a fairly big man. I looked like a teamster, uncomfortable in the tie I'd stuck on for the labor negotiations. I looked a bit like my dad, which was both reassuring and disturbing. We agreed that I definitely looked like a straight man. John Goodman-esque. There was no doubt that I could pass, provided I kept my mouth shut.

Now that I was dressed for action, it was time to figure out where to find it. I reminded myself about Diane Torr, a drag king and perfor-mance artist who has gone into Muslim countries and brought veiled women into the streets as men to experience life from a perspective forbidden to them. I, too, wanted to go where no woman had gone be-fore. I wanted to go someplace that I could absolutely never see as a woman, some inner sanctum of masculinity. I could go to a gay bar but that would be inviting the scrutiny of experts. I could go to a topless bar but there was really nothing forbidden about that. My dresser came up with the perfect suggestion: The "buddy booths" of midtown Man-hattan. Men went to these places for anonymous oral sex; what on earth were my socks and I going to do there?

We drove across town to one of the few places that former New York City Mayor Rudolph Giuliani's "quality of life" campaign had ap-parently missed; perhaps this was part of a separate "quality of porn" initiative? Ostensibly a XXX video store, through a curtained doorway lay a back room with all the aesthetic charm of a public bathroom. Pic-ture the same rickety stalls, doors reaching neither to floor nor to frame, with all of the gaps and cracks one ordinarily finds embarrass-ing. There, though, it was part of the point.

Inside each stall was a seat and a video screen. The screen accepted quarters; each one bought you a two-minute clip of hardcore pornogra-phy. The videos, however, were not the real attraction. The walls be-tween the booths were equipped with curtained windows; if men in ad-joining booths decided to raise their curtains, both got an extra show for free. What's more, the regulars knew that these Plexiglas windows were not actually secured in place. One could work one's fingers in around the bottom edge of a window and lift it up a few inches, allow-ing safe passage for one's penis into the next guy's booth. Leave the curtain down and raise the window and you never had to see your part-ner. That's perfect if you prefer to remain anonymous. No doubt it was the cheapest blowjob in town.

What kind of men went to the buddy booths? Let's just say they ap-peared to be straight. In other words: Their clothes were boring. Yet they were engaging in homosexual behavior. At the time, gay men knew that they could go to a bar and have anonymous sex for free; they didn't need to plug quarters into a slot in a simulated toilet stall. But a man who wanted to avoid thinking of himself as gay might have preferred the anonymity of a buddy booth, where he could come and go like a sneeze. Indeed, the men I saw there looked largely like I did, straight and uncomfortable.

It was a delicate dance that I witnessed there, a wordless agreement made only with the eyes. I was struck by the silence. Men stood in corners, leaning against surfaces, their eyes darting from face to face and crotch to crotch, seeking signs. Somehow they communicated exactly who was going to do what to whom with just one direct look. Two men entered adjoining booths; others stole glances at them between the cracks. They can do whatever they want inside as long as they both keep plugging quarters into the video machines. Every so often the owner comes back to rap on a door, insisting the occupant leave or spend money.

There I stood, socks bulging. Like a check you can't cash. There was no way I was going into any of the booths for a closer examination. I could hardly see through the cracks and still I saw more than I wanted to. Eventually I became aware that someone was stealing glances at me: a tall, middle aged man who looked like he might be an accountant. He tried repeatedly to meet my eyes but I kept averting them. Scared at first, my initial impulse was to bolt. Was I afraid of being discovered, or only of my own sudden desire to see the fantasy through to its end? My personality fractured. The dyke was disgusted, but the man within me had a hard-on. I knew exactly what my voyeur wanted. In the fractions of seconds that his eyes met mine, he communicated his desires precisely. Surely he would have lifted the glass and knelt before me if only Pinocchio had been real. I walked into another room to break the tension.

Feigning interest, I focused intensely on the boxed videos, hoping my admirer would get the message. Less than a minute passed before he took a stall next to a fellow even beefier than me; immediately I felt a flash of jealousy. Well, I consoled myself, at least he was attracted to me first. I left the place and went to a McDonald's where I cut in front of two women in line. They smiled and deferred, taking two steps back. I laughed inwardly, feeling mean and powerful, and instantly felt regret. I ordered food I knew I wouldn't eat and gave it to a startled homeless man a few blocks later.

The drag kings were curious about my experience. I think they expected I'd be drawn to it like they were, that I'd want to do it all the time, come up with an act of my own and compete with them for gigs. They knew how seductive it was, this lesbian ownership of maleness. But it didn't appeal to me as I had feared it might. If anything, it served at the time to anchor me more solidly to my butch, female identity. While passing as a man gave me the gift of male privilege, it came at a cost too high to bear: Women feared me. They crossed streets to avoid me. I treated them rudely and they allowed it. No self-respecting butch could live with that.

It took me a long time to realize that I hadn't been acting like a man; I had been acting like an asshole. The advice the drag kings had given me was so over-the-top that no man in my life actually conformed to it. I suppose if they had gone on stage and acted like my dad, then it wouldn't have been very entertaining: Picture a salesman on his feet eight hours a day, six days a week, miserable in his job but committed to keeping it in order to support his family. Drag is not about that. Drag is about making fun of masculinity by exaggerating it. It's about subverting the established order by covertly seizing male privilege. In any case, it's profoundly different from being male identified. When I was in drag I felt like a fraud.

I'm not a man and I never will be. It's too late for that. I'm not a woman and I never was. I spent a lifetime trying and enough is enough. If my body matched my brain then it would be male, and if that had happened in utero, then I would have been raised as a boy and grown up to be a man. Instead, I have lived my life as if I were a male inconvenienced by the fact of a female body, which I have expected everyone else to ignore as much as I do. This caused me to hate myself. Invisibly but profoundly, and always.

The only way forward is through. I am a transman.

28

Concluding Thoughts

Life is most transfixing when you are awake to diversity, not only of ethnicity, ability, gender, belief, and sexuality but also of age and experience. The worst mistake anyone can make is to perceive anyone else as lesser. ~ Andrew Solomon, (2015, para. 2)

✦✦✦

The stories of transmasculine individuals are many—too many to include in this book, and there are far more facets of being trans than one book could possibly cover. Some of stories told in the questionnaires and in emails I have received from trans individuals at various points in their journeys are heartbreaking.

Stories like those recounting the bullying, harassment, and hate they have faced, such as these individuals have shared:

I was bullied all through childhood until I graduated high school for who I am. I was beat up, verbally harassed, threatened with sexual abuse, spat on, teased, etc (21, Male/Man)

I was bashed more as a lesbian. This didn't make me want to transition any more or less...it just made me angry. This has had an impact on my performance of masculinity, for sure. (44, FTM)

The hate from family and Christians made me question myself many times and I still do. I believe in God and hope that this is a part of my experience on Earth and that I was meant to face and overcome it. I still question myself though and the suffering I have brought on my family and the suffering I might cause my cis male partner through his family and often wonder if detransitioning would be the right thing. I know it would mean death for me though. (28, Male/Man)

I have been told that I am not trans enough, that I am an abomination. That I am a freak. I should suck it up and be female. (20, Transman)

I have had to prove I didn't steal my own identity due to name and gender change. I've been hassled at medical providers- heard disparaging remarks, had health care claims denied. (48, Male/Man)

There are the fears, the low self-esteem, suicidal thoughts and self-harm that are so common to many trans individuals;

I am not a classic manly man. I wonder whether I will ever get the courage to do medical transition. Sometimes I feel like I'm failing, like I failed at being a woman, and now I'm failing at being trans, too. That doesn't help my self-esteem. (28, Transgender)

I frequently feel disgusted by my own body. I want to change it, but exercise requires wearing gym clothes and not wearing a binder, and I feel naked. (18, Genderqueer)

I decided to come out as trans-masculine after getting treatment for depression and anxiety following a suicide attempt at age 16. I was deeply depressed and I'd thought seriously of suicide since I was 12. As I started getting therapy I began talking about my gender identity and how uncomfortable I became with my body as I went through puberty. It had become clear to me that I had more life to live in front of me, whether I wanted it or not. I came out to some close friends, and co-founded the QSU (Queer Student Union) at my high school. (18, Genderfluid)

I had debilitating dysphoria that lead to suicidal ideation and suicide attempts. (21, Male/Man)

Gosh going on road trips and having to drive through rural Kansas and missouri and Idaho and feeling very unsafe presenting masculine. I even found myself dressing more femme to deal with the amount of hatred I felt from strangers. (29, Genderqueer)

I've been self-harming for close to four years now. It's not constant, and mostly I have ceased, but there are some days where I break down. And that may be from stress, dysphoria, panic attacks, and when I break down, it's almost impossible for me to calm down without putting a few fresh cuts on my stomach. For a while I would stop, and it was replaced with (safely) stretching my ear lobes, because it is something that only I can control and stretching to bigger sizes can sometimes bring a small amount of pain (cutting provides similar feelings of control, only with more pain). Stretching my ears has been my main variable now, and cutting more infrequently, but they both still hold a grip throughout this high school transgender experience. (16, Genderfluid)

My self-esteem was extremely low. I was too fat, too ugly or too whatever. During my transition, it got worse before it got better. I started feeling more paranoid about who I was. Whether I would pass next to other men. Whether I was masculine enough. (26, FTM)

There were those, too, who highlighted the problem of discrimination *within* the trans community—those who took issue with Genderqueer and non-binary people:

I don't think genderqueer belongs with transgender movement. I don't feel that genderqueer\gender fluid has anything to do with masculinity. There is a lot more to being a man than facial hair or standing to pee. (58, Transman)

Honestly - this confuses the crap out of me. I don't get it. At all. And I get annoyed at trying to keep up with the various pronouns people want used. If you look like a man, don't get angry when someone calls you "he" on the street and lecture them. How the hell are we supposed to know? Seems like everyone in the gender fluid movement walks around with a giant chip on their shoulder just waiting to bite someone's head off while correcting them. (40, Transman)

I think some genderqueer people should back up and make more space for transgender voices. I think there are privilege issues where genderqueer people have more privilege and act like they don't and that is annoying. (55, Genderqueer)

And those who were the victims of this intergroup discrimination...

I don't know what to say about this other than I don't understand the resistance and hatred I relieve from so many binary trans folks. Strange and sad. (39, Non-binary)

There were a few...that said I "wasn't trans enough" because I did not act masculine. I was shunned by the majority of the FTM trans community in my area for a while. I wound up feeling forced back into the closet and I hid the fact that I was trans again and went back to looking girly for 7 months. Since then they have apologized and I have made a point to make sure no one else in this area is ever shunned again for being themselves. (27, Bi-gender)

These statements do not fully envelope the full transmasculine experience. They do, however, indicate there is still a long, hard road ahead for those who are actively trying to effect changes in legislation as well as those working to change hearts and minds of people in their churches, schools, medical institutions, and local businesses.

❀ ❀ ❀

The purpose of this book is to help inform readers of the multitude of experiences, genders, sexualities, beliefs and values found within the transmasculine community. It is my fervent hope that in learning more in-depth the diversity found within the community, there will be more acceptance, inclusiveness and cohesion in a group of individuals who have all struggled at some point in their lives to be heard, recognized and validated for who they are.

We make assumptions every day about other people's genders without ever seeing their birth certificates, their chromosomes, their genitals, their reproductive systems, their childhood socialization, or their legal sex. There is no such thing as a "real" gender - there is only the gender we experience ourselves as and the gender we perceive other to be. ~ Julia Serano (2009, p. 13).

⬥⬥⬥ The End ⬥⬥⬥

Glossary

Androgynous: The quality exhibited by people who are difficult to identify as either clearly male or clearly female, and may have characteristics of both male and female. Some trans people whose genders cannot be classified as strictly male or strictly female call themselves androgynes. Also known as Androgyny.

Binary Gender System: A culturally defined code of acceptable behaviors which teach that there only two and only two distinct states of gender, men and women, who are masculine and feminine.

Binding: The process of flattening one's breasts to have a more masculine or flat appearing chest.

Bottom Surgery: Surgery on the genitals designed to create a body in harmony with a person's preferred gender expression.

Butch: Butch is a word commonly used in the lesbian and gay communities to identify masculine females or sometimes masculine gay men. The spectrum of identity within the lesbian community can include "soft butches" who identify masculine women, to transgender butches who often do not identify as "women" and are somewhat bi-gendered in their identity," to those who identify as transmen/FTM's but still retain an identity as "butch."

Cisgender: A term used by some to describe people who are not transgender. "Cis-" is a Latin prefix meaning "on the same side as," and is therefore an antonym of "trans-."

Coming Out: Announcing to your family, friends or work associates some previously secret aspect of your sexual or gender identity.

Detransition: halting or reversing a decision to change sex.

Drag King: Used to refer to female or trans men performers who dress as men for the purposes of entertaining others at bars, clubs, or other events. Typically involves exaggerated performance of gendered characteristics.

Feminism: The advocacy of women's rights on the grounds of political, social, and economic equality to men; the belief that women should have equal rights and opportunities

Fluid(ity): Generally describes an identity that is a fluctuating mix of the options available (e.g., man and woman, gay and straight); not to be confused with "transitioning"

FTM: A person who transitions from "female-to-male," meaning a person who was assigned female at birth, but identifies and lives as a male. It is not claimed by all transmasculine individuals due to its binary connotations. Also, many do not believe they were ever "female," so there is no "transition" in the respect of female to male.

Gender Expression: How a person represents or expresses one's gender identity to others, often through behavior, clothing, hairstyles, voice or body characteristics.

Gender Identity: An individual's internal sense of being male, female, or something else. Since gender identity is internal, one's gender identity is not necessarily visible to others.

Gender Non-Conforming: A term used to describe some people whose gender expression is different from conventional expectations of masculinity and femininity. Not all gender non-conforming people identify as transgender; nor are all transgender people gender non-conforming. The term is not a synonym for transgender or transsexual and should only be used if someone self-identifies as gender non-conforming.

Gender Oppression: The societal, institutional, and individual beliefs and practices that privilege cisgender (gender-typical people) and subordinate and disparage transgender or gender variant people. Also known as "genderism."

Gender role: Describes the set of expectations that are ascribed to a certain gender in any given culture, relating to how to people of that gender "should" (among other things) behave, talk, dress, and think.

Genderqueer: A term used by some individuals who identify as neither entirely male nor entirely female. These are generally individuals who do not-- or will not -- adhere to the expectation of the only two gender presentations that which our culture allows.

Hegemony: preponderant influence or authority over others; the social, cultural, ideological, or economic influence exerted by a dominant group

Herstory: history viewed from a female or specifically feminist perspective.

Hormone Replacement Therapy: Medical treatment using hormones, used by transsexuals to affect the development of secondary sex characteristics such as developing breasts. In non-transsexual individuals, the use of hormones is most-often used to treat the discomforts of menopause or to replace hormones (especially estrogen) lost after menopause.

HRT: See Hormone Replacement Therapy

Intersex: A term used for people who are born with a reproductive or sexual anatomy and/or chromosome pattern that does not seem to fit typical definitions of male or female.

Lesbian: A dictionary definition includes "of or relating to homosexual women or to homosexuality in women." Generally a term used by women, although there are transmasculine individuals who claim it as an identity because it is more suitable than other current terminologies.

Male Privilege: A concept for examining social, economic, and political advantages or rights that are made available to men solely on the basis of their sex. A man's access to these benefits may also depend on other characteristics such as race, sexual orientation and social class.

Misogyny: the hatred and denigration of women and characteristics deemed feminine.

Non-binary: Non-binary people are those who don't feel male or female. They may feel like both or like something in between. They may have a gender that changes over time or they may not relate to gender at all.

Omnisexual: A person who is attracted to all people regardless of their sex or gender.

Oppression: is the inequitable use of authority, law, or physical force to prevent others from being free or equal. *Gendered oppression* is the systemic manner in which certain groups are privileged or disadvantaged because of their gender. Intersects with discrimination based on race, sexuality, ability, class, age, history of incarceration, religion, language, and citizenship status.

Packing: Wearing a phallic device on the groin and under clothing for any purposes including: (for someone without a biological penis) the validation or confirmation of one's masculine gender identity; seduction; and/or sexual readiness (for one who likes to penetrate another during sexual intercourse).

Pansexual: A person who is sexually attracted to all or many gender expressions.

Pass: To be accepted without question in your chosen gender. The term has a problematic history and connotation, as some people believe that "passing" denotes a deception—a way of "fooling" others.
Queer: A term used to refer to lesbian, gay, bisexual and, often also transgender, people. Depending on the context, the term can be either a derogatory or affirming, as there are those in the LGBT community have sought to reclaim the term that was once widely used in a negative way. Not everyone agrees with its use or identifies with this term.

Patriarchy: A system of society or government in which men hold the power and women are largely excluded from it.

Presentation: The totality of one's appearance when dressing, including voice, behavior, appropriateness of clothing for the situation, etc.

Sexism: Discrimination based on gender, especially discrimination against women; the belief that one gender is superior to the other, especially that men are superior to women.

Sexual Orientation: A term describing a person's attraction to members physical attraction to others—can be lesbian, gay, bisexual, pansexual, omnisexual, asexual,

Sexual Reassignment Surgery (SRS): A term used by some medical professionals to refer to a group of surgical options that alter a person's "sex". In most states, one or multiple surgeries are required to achieve legal recognition of gender variance. Also known as "Gender Confirming Surgery," or the lesser used "Gender Reassignment Surgery"

Stealth: This term refers to when a person chooses to be secretive about their gender history, either after transitioning or while successful passing.

Stereotype: A preconceived or oversimplified generalization about an entire group of people without regard for their individual differences. Though often negative, can also be complimentary. Even positive stereotypes can have a negative impact, however, simply because they involve broad generalizations that ignore individual realities.

Testosterone (T): The hormone that is essential for sperm production and the development of male characteristics, including muscle mass and strength, fat distribution, bone mass, facial hair growth, voice change and sex drive.

Third Gender: Someone who does not identify with the traditional genders of "man" or "woman" but identifies with another gender; it is a gender category available in some countries that recognize three or more genders.

Top Surgery: For trans men, top surgery refers to removal of the breasts. Also known as Chest Reconstruction Surgery.

Trans Butch: Signifies a gendered embodiment that is both butch and trans, not tied to any singular definition of butch or trans but rather falling somewhere in between. The individual may identify as male or female, and may or may not identify as lesbian.

Transgender: A term for people whose gender identity, expression or behavior is different from those typically associated with their assigned sex at birth. Transgender is a broad term and is good for non-transgender people to use.

Transmasculine: A term used to describe transgender people who were assigned female at birth, but identify with masculinity to a greater extent than with femininity.

Transmasculine Butch: Similar to Trans Butch, with the individual clearly identifying as more masculine than feminine. Generally adopted by trans men, but can also be claimed by masculine lesbians.

Transmisogyny: Negative attitudes expressed through cultural hate, individual and state violence, and discrimination directed toward trans and gender non-conforming people.

Transphobia: Discrimination of and negative attitudes toward transgender people based on their gender expression.

Transition: The time when a person begins to living as the gender with which they identify rather than the gender they were assigned at birth, which often, but not always, includes changing one's name, and perhaps dressing or expressing their outward presentation differently. Transitioning may or may not also include medical and legal aspects, including taking hormones, having surgery, or changing identity documents (e.g. driver's license, Social Security record) to reflect one's gender identity.

Transsexual: An older term for people whose gender identity is different from their assigned sex at birth who seeks to physically transition from male to female or female to male. Not all are able to afford a medical transition. Many do not prefer this term because it is binary in nature, and is exclusive of all gender non-conforming people.

Womyn: Womyn is one of a number of alternate spellings of the word "woman" which some (especially some feminists) promote as a way to remove the perception of gender bias from the English word women.

References

Abelson, M. (2014). Men in Context: Transmasculinities and Transgender Experiences in Three US Regions. (Dissertation, University of Oregon).

Agency. (2016). Winner of National Transgender Beauty Pageant Stripped of Her Title Because She Was 'Not Transgender Enough'. *Telegraph Media Group Limited*. Retrieved from http://www.telegraph.co.uk/news /uknews/12165845/Winner-of-national-transgender-beauty-pageant-stripped-of-her-title-because-she-was-not-transgender-enough.html

Berlatsky, N. (2014). Can Men Really Be Feminists? *The Atlantic Monthly Group*. Retrieved from http://www.theatlantic.com/national/archive/2014/06/men-can-be-feminists-too/372234/

Best, D. L. (2003). Gender Stereotypes. In C. Ember & M. Ember (Eds.), *Encyclopedia of Sex and Gender: Men and Women in the World's Cultures*. Dordrecht, The Netherlands: Springer Science + Business Media.

Bornstein, K. (1994). *Gender Outlaw: Of Men, Women, and the Rest of Us*. New York: Vintage.

Bornstein, K. (1998). *My Gender Workbook*. New York: Routledge.

Bornstein, K., & Bergman, S. B. (2010). *Gender Outlaws: The Next Generation*. Seal Press.

Brown, M.E. (2015). *Pencil Me In: A Trans Perspective in a Gendered World*. Miami, Florida: Boundless Endeavors, Inc.

Burke, P.J. & Tully, J. (1977). The Measurement of Role/ Identity. *Social Forces, 55*. (880-897).

Burke, P. J. (1991). Identity Processes and Social Stress. *American Sociological Review*, 836-849.

Butler, J. (1988). Performative Acts and Gender Constitution: An Essay in Phenomenology and Feminist Theory. *Theatre Journal, 40*(4), 519–531. http://doi.org/10.2307 /3207893

Connell, R.W. (1995). *Masculinities*. Berkeley: University of California Press.

Connell, R.W. (1996). Teaching the Boys: New Research on Masculinity, and Gender Strategies for Schools. *The Teachers College Record*, 98(2), 206-235.

Connell, R. W., & Messerschmidt, J. W. (2005). Hegemonic Masculinity Rethinking the Concept. *Gender & Society, 19*(6), 829-859.

Cook-Daniels, L. (1999). Femmes, Butches and Lesbian-Feminists Discussing FTMs. *FORGE.*

Creighton, S. (2001). Surgery For Intersex. *Journal of the Royal Society of Medicine, 94*(5), 218-220.

Currie, G., & Rothenberg, C. (2002). *Feminist Revisions of the Subject: Landscapes, Ethnoscapes, and Theoryscapes.* Lexington Books.

Devor, H. (1989). *Gender Blending: Confronting the Limits of Duality* (Vol. 533). Indiana University Press.

Devor, H. (1997) *FTM: Female to Male Transsexuals In Society.* Bloomington: Indiana University Press, 1997.

Devor, H. (2002). Who Are "We"? Where Sexual Orientation Meets Gender Identity. *Journal of Gay & Lesbian Psychotherapy, 6*(2), 5-21.

Dictionary.com. (2016). "Misogyny". Dictionary.com, LLC. Retrieved from http://dictionary.reference.com/browse/misogyny

Dictionary.com. (2016). "Privilege". Dictionary.com, LLC. Retrieved from http://dictionary.reference.com/ browse/privilege

Dozier, R. (2005). Beards, Breasts, and Bodies Doing Sex in a Gendered World. *Gender & Society, 19*(3), 297-316. DOI: 10.1177/0891243204272153

Duffy, N. (2016). Trans Beauty Queen Was Stripped of Crown for 'Not Being Transgender Enough'. *Pink News.* Retrieved from http://www.pinknews.co.uk/ 2016/02/19/trans-beauty-queen-was-stripped-of-crown-for-not-being-transgender-enough/

Elliot, P. (2004). Who Gets to Be a Woman?: Feminist Politics and the Question of Trans-inclusion. *Atlantis: Critical Studies in Gender, Culture & Social Justice, 29*(1), 13.

Faderman, L. (1991*). Odd Girls and Twilight Lovers: A History of Lesbian Life in Twentieth Century America.* New York: Columbia University Press.

Feinberg, L. (1992). Transgender Liberation: A Movement Whose Time Has Come. In C. McCann & S.K. Kim (Eds.) *Feminist Theory Reader: Local and Global Perspectives.* Routledge.

Feinberg, L. (2006) Transmissions—Interview With Leslie Feinberg. *Camp Magazine.* Retrieved from http://www. campkc.com/campkc-content.php?Page_ID=225

Firestone, S. (1970). *The Dialectic of Sex: The Case for Feminist Revolution.* New York: Farrar, Straus and Girroux

Forshee, A.S. (2006). Perceptions of Masculinity Among Transgender

Men . (Doctoral dissertation). ProQuest.

Forshee, A. S. (2008). Transgender Men: A Demographic Snapshot. *Journal of Gay & Lesbian Social Services, 20*(3), 331–236. doi:10.1080/10538720802235229

Fournier, V. L., & Smith, W. (2006). Scripting Masculinity. *Ephemera, 6*(2), pp. 141-162.

Freire, P. (1993). *Pedagogy of the Oppressed.* New York: Continuum

Gately, C. (2010). *Solidarity in the Borderlands of Gender, Race, Class and Sexuality: Racialized Transgender Men* (Doctoral dissertation, University of Toronto).

Gender. (2015). *World Health Organization.* Retrieved from http://www.who.int/mediacentre/factsheets/ fs403/en/

Glotfelter, M. A. (2012). Undergraduate Students' Gender Self-Esteem and Attitudes Towards Transmen, Transwomen, Gay Men, and Lesbian Women. (Dissertation, Indiana State University.

Grant, J.M., Mottet, L.A. & Tanis, J. (2009). Executive Summary. Injustice at Every Turn: A Report of the National Transgender Discrimination Survey. *National Gay and Lesbian Task Force and the National Center for Transgender Equality.*

Green, J. (1998). FTM: An Emerging Voice, in Dallas Denny (Ed.), *Current Concepts in Transgender Identity*, (p. 152). New York: Garland Publishing.

Green, J. (2004). *Becoming a Visible Man.* New Hampshire: Vanderbilt University Press.

Green, J. (2005). Part of the Package: Ideas of Masculinity Among Male-Identified Transpeople. *Men and Masculinities, 7*(3), 291–299. doi:10.1177/1097184X04272116

Green, E. R. (2006). Debating Trans Inclusion in the Feminist Movement: A Trans-Positive Analysis. *Journal of lesbian studies, 10*(1-2), 231-248.

Halberstam, Jude. (1998a). *Female Masculinity.* Durham: Duke University Press.

Halberstam, J. (1998b). Transgender Butch: Butch/FTM Border Wars and the Masculine Continuum. *GLQ: A Journal of Lesbian and Gay Studies, 4*(2), 287-310.

Hale, C. Jacob. (1998). Tracing a Ghostly Memory in My Throat: Reflections on Ftm Feminist Voice and Agency. In T. Digby (Ed.), *Men Doing Feminism* (pp. 99-129). New York: Routledge.

Hall, K. (2014). Create a Sense of Belonging. *Psychology Today.* Retrieved from https://www.psychologytoday.com/blog /pieces-mind/201403/create-sense-belonging

Hansbury, G. (2002). Testosterone Transcript. *This American Life*. Retrieved from http://www.thisamericanlife.org/radio-archives/episode/220/transcript

Hansbury, G. (2005). Mourning the Loss of the Idealized Self: A Transsexual Passage. *Psychoanalytic Social Work, 12*(1), 19-35.

Hansbury, G. (2005). The Middle Men: An Introduction to the Transmasculine Identities. *Studies in Gender and Sexuality, 6*(3), 241-264.

Haynes, F., & McKenna, T. (Eds.). (2001). *Unseen Genders: Beyond the Binaries* (Vol. 12). Peter Lang Pub Incorporated.

Herstory. (n.d.). In *Merriam-Webster.com*. Retrieved from http://www.merriam-webster.com/dictionary/herstory

hooks, b. (2000). *Feminism is For Everybody: Passionate politics*. Pluto Press.

How Common is Intersex? (n.d.). *Intersex Society of North America*. Retrieved from http://www.isna.org /faq/frequency

Jeanes, E., Knights, D., & Martin, P. Y. (Eds.). (2012). *Handbook of Gender, Work and Organization*. John Wiley & Sons.

Johnson, A.G. (2005). *The Gender Knot: Unraveling Our Patriarchal Legacy*. Philadelphia, PA: Temple University Press.

Kacere, L. (2014). Transmisogyny 101: What It Is and What Can We Do About It. *Everyday Feminism*. Retrieved from http://everyday-feminism.com/2014/01/transmisogyny/

Kallahan, K. (2014). Forced Femininity Saved My Life: One Genderqueer on Male 'Privilege'. Jezebel. Retrieved from http://roygbiv.jezebel.com/forced-femininity-saved-my-life-one-genderqueer-on-mal-1665956295?utm_campaign=socialflow_jezebel_facebook&utm_source= jezebel_facebook&utm_medium=socialflow

Kanter, R.M. (2013). Is Tribalism Inevitable? *Huffington Post*. Retrieved from http://www.huffingtonpost.com/rosabeth-moss-kanter/is-tribalism-inevitable_b_3661436.html

Lenning, E. (2009). Moving Beyond the Binary: Exploring the Dimensions of Gender Presentation and Orientation. *International Journal of Social Inquiry, 2*(2), 39-54.

Lerner, G. (1986). *The Creation of Patriarchy*. New York, NY: Oxford University Press.

Levitt, H. M., & Hiestand, K. R. (2004). A Quest for Authenticity: Contemporary Butch Gender. *Sex Roles, 50*(9-10), 605-621.

Manion, J. (2014). Transbutch. *TSQ: Transgender Studies Quarterly*, 1(1-2), 230-232.

Maslow, A. (1954). *Motivation and Personality*. New York: Harper.

Merriam-Webster. (2015) "Hegemony". *Merriam-Webster, Incorporated.* Retrieved from http://www.merriam-webster.com/dictionary/hegemony

Mikkola, M. (2016). "Feminist Perspectives on Sex and Gender", in *The Stanford Encyclopedia of Philosophy*, Zalta, E.N. (Ed). Retrieved from http://plato.stanford.edu/archives/fall2012/entries/feminism-gender/.

Mills, J. (1989). *Womanwords a Vocabulary of Culture and Patriarchal Society.* Virago Press Ltd.

Money, J., Hampson, J. G., & Hampson, J. L. (1955). An examination of some basic sexual concepts: the evidence of human hermaphroditism. *Bulletin of the Johns Hopkins Hospital, 97*(4), 301.

Morgan, R. (2014). *The Word of a Woman: Feminist Dispatches.* Open Road Media.

Munroe, R. L.; Munroe, R. H. (1975/1994). *Cross-Cultural Human Development.* Waveland Press Prospect Heights, IL.

Neufeld, C. (2008). Lost in Transition. *Calvinneuveld.com.* Retrieved from http://www.calvinneufeld.com/2011/ 07/lost-in-transition.html

Nicholson, L. (1994). Interpreting Gender. *Signs*, 79–105.

Noble, JB. (2006). *Sons of the Movement: FTMs Risking Incoherence on a Post ¬Queer Cultural Landscape.* Toronto: Women's Press

Oakley, A. (2015). *Sex, Gender and Society.* Ashgate Publishing, Ltd.

Oxford Dictionary. (2016). "Ally" & "Feminist". *Oxford University Press.*

Prince, V. (2005). Sex vs. gender. *International Journal of Transgenderism, 8*(4), 29–32. (Original work published 1973).

Rands, K. E. (2009). Considering Transgender People in Education: A Gender-Complex Approach. *Journal of Teacher Education, 60*(4), 419-431.

Raymond, J. G. (1980). *The Transsexual Empire.* Women's Press.

Rex, M.A. (2016) Featured Voices: The First 7 Days. *Neutrois Nonsense.* Retrieved from http://neutrois.me/2016/02/ 27/fv-top-surgery-7-days/

Ridgeway, C. & Correll, S.J. (2004). Unpacking the Gender System: A Theoretical Perspective on Gender Beliefs and Social Relations. *Gender & Society, 18*(4), 510-531.

Rubin, G. (1992). Of Catamites and Kings. Reflections on Butch, Gender, and Boundaries. In *Transgender Studies Reader*, ed. Susan Stryker and Stephen Whittle. New York: Routledge, 2006.

Safir, M. P., Rosenmann, A., & Kloner, O. (2003). Tomboyism, Sexual Orientation, and Adult Gender Roles Among Israeli Women. *Sex*

Roles, 48, 401–410.

Sachs, A. (2011). "From Chasity to Chaz: Sonny and Cher's Child on His Sex-Change Operation". Time Inc. Retrieved from http://content.time.com/time/arts/ article/0,8599,2070191,00.html

SAMSHA. Addressing the Specific Behavioral Health Needs of Men. *Substance Abuse and Mental Health Services.* Administration. Retrieved from http://www.ncbi.nlm.nih.gov/ books/NBK144300/

Schifter, J. & Madrigal, J. (2000). *The Sexual Construction of Latino Youth: Implications For the Spread of HIV/AIDS.* New York: The Haworth Hispanic/Latino Press.

Seidler, V. J. (2006). *Transforming Masculinities: Men, Cultures, Bodies, Power, Sex and Love.* London & New York: Taylor & Francis.

Serano, J. (2009). *Whipping girl: A transsexual woman on sexism and the scapegoating of femininity.* Seal Press.

Shadden, C. (2016) Social Inequality and Marginalization of Transgender Individuals. *The Corinthian, 16.*

Sibley, C. G., Overall, N. C., & Duckitt, J. (2007). When Women Become More Hostilely Sexist Toward Their Gender: The System-Justifying Effect of Benevolent Sexism. *Sex Roles, 57*(9-10), 743-754.

Solomon, A. (2015). The Middle of Things: Advice For Young Writers. *The New Yorker.* Retrieved from http://www.newyorker.com/books/page-turner/the-middle-of-things-advice-for-young-writers

Stoller, R. J. (1968) *Sex and Gender: On The Development of Masculinity and Femininity.* New York: Science House.

Stryker, S. (2008). *Transgender History.* Seal Press.

Stryker, S. (2014). Biopolitics. *TSQ: Transgender Studies Quarterly, 1*(1-2), 38-42.

Substance Abuse and Mental Health Services Administration (SAMHSA). (2013). Addressing the Specific Behavioral Needs of Men. *U.S. Department of Health and Human Services.* PDF.

Weigert, A. J., Teitge, J. S., & Teitge, D. W. (2007). *Society and Identity: Toward a Sociological Psychology.* Cambridge University Press.

Weiss, J. T. (2007). The Lesbian Community and FTMs: Détente in the Butch/FTM Borderlands. *Journal of lesbian studies, 11*(3-4), 203-211.

West, C., & Zimmerman, D. H. (2009). Accounting for doing gender. *Gender & Society,* 112-122.

White, M. (1996). Men's culture, the men's movement, and the constitution of men's lives. *Men's ways of being*, 163-194. Boulder, CO: Westview Press

Whittle, S. (2000) *The Transgender Debate: The Crisis Surrounding Gender Identities*. Reading, South Street Press.

Williams, R. (1977). *Marxism and Literature*. London: Oxford University Press.

Winter, S. (2010). Lost in transition: Transpeople, Transprejudice and Pathology in Asia. In P. C. W. Chan (Ed.), *Protection of Sexual Minorities Since Stonewall: Progress and Stalemate in Developed and Developing Countries*. (pp. 231-256). New York, NY: Routledge/Taylor & Francis Group

Wolchover, N. (2012). Why Is Pink for Girls and Blue for Boys? *LiveScience.com*. Retrieved from http://www. livescience.com/22037-pink-girls-blue-boys.html

Wood, J. T. (2013). Ch. 1 The Study of Communication, Gender and Culture. *Gendered Lives: Communication, Gender, and Culture* (10th ed.). Belmont, Calif.: Cengage Learning

Zimman, L. *Transmasculinity and the Voice: Gender Assignment, Identity, and Presentation*. Retrieved from http://lalzimman.com/papers/Zimman2015a.pdf

Zitz, C., Burns, J., & Tacconelli, E. (2014). Trans Men and Friendships: A Foucauldian Discourse Analysis. *Feminism & Psychology*, DOI:0959353514526224.

About the Author

Michael Eric Brown is the Founder and Executive Director of Trans-Mentors International, Inc., a non-profit organization dedicated to supporting transgender men, women and youth in their day-to-day lives. He is known for his contributions both on and offline, especially in the realm of social justice and gender concerns. A student who is interested in how people's thoughts, feelings, and behaviors are influenced by the actual, imagined, or implied presence of others, Michael is working his way towards a PhD in Social Psychology in order to both educate society and provide research on the lives of transgender individuals. As a professional freelance writer, he writes on a variety of subjects and engages his readers with his unique writing style.

Also By This Author

Pencil Me In: A Trans Perspective in a Gendered World
Copyright© 2015 Michael Eric Brown

Michael Eric Brown shares not only his personal life as a transgender man, but he also talks candidly about gender roles and societal expectations. Approaching the subjects with frankness and occasional humor, he shares his experiences as well as those of countless others in the transgender community in order to communicate openly what it means to be a transgender individual in today's society.

This book presents a straight-forward examination of definitions and perceptions of gender roles and expectations, and the oppression transgender people are forced to overcome due to these expectations. Covering areas such as the language of gender, feminist views, oppression and more, Michael approaches the subject of being transgender in a world that is still struggling to acknowledge that gender really isn't just a black and white binary concept. He applies personal examples, observations and statistics in order to enlighten and educate in an informative and reader-friendly style.

Pencil Me In was written in small increments over several years and ultimately the pieces have become chapters in the book. Michael shares his experiences of growing up as a victim of Munchausen by Proxy from his drug-addicted mother, incest, overcoming intense anger issues and the years of healing and self-discoveries to finally become the person he is now.

WHAT PEOPLE ARE SAYING

"In Michael Eric Brown's latest book, *Pencil Me In*, he leads us through the challenges and triumphs of his life and transition from a man trapped inside the body of a genetic female. His struggles through childhood physical and sexual abuse, psychological turmoil, drug use and trying to fit into the lesbian world are all remarkable, but not as much as his path to finding peace and happiness as a man. People interested in gender, others who are faced with their own, or a loved one's transition, and therapists/ academics who wish to understand and share the insider's view of the gendered world will find this book a necessity." – David S Bathory, PsyD, Bathory International, Specialist in LBGTQI & Trauma

"Everyone who is trans or gender questioning, or has family that is or works with these interesting people should read this book that gives such good advice and insight into our changing world." – Just Evelyn, Author, *"Mom, I Need to be a Girl"*

Pencil Me In: A Trans Perspective in a Gendered World is available in Paperback and digital editions at Amazon and other online retailers.

www.ingramcontent.com/pod-product-compliance
Lightning Source LLC
Chambersburg PA
CBHW052126270326
41930CB00012B/2774